FLYING BY THE SEATS OF THEIR SKIRTS:
POWERFUL STORIES CENTERED
IN KINDNESS BY INSPIRING WOMEN

To my most inspiring sister. Thankyou for being such a beautiful light & being part of my story from now until forever. ♥

2019

net(worlding
PUBLISHING

Flying by the Seats of Their Skirts:
Powerful Stories Centered in Kindness by Inspiring Women
Print: 978-1-944027-38-4
Copyright ©2019 by Networlding Publishing

DEDICATION

This book is dedicated to all of you who strive to make the world a kinder and better place for all women. My intention for you is to attain total abundance, joy, kindness and love for you for your entire existence.

TABLE OF CONTENTS

FOREWORD

In today's over-busy world, when women are filling more professional roles than ever before, often there's not enough time to share our *real* personal stories—those stories that make us who we are and how we show up in the world. We don't really get to hear about how other women see themselves, or what they've gone through to get to where they are today. There are so many social media channels with unrealistic snippets of a "perfect moment" but not real meaningful stories being told. I wanted to change that.

This book was uniquely initiated in real time through a one-day collaborative writing effort. Here, supported by a cutting-edge book creation expert, Melissa G Wilson, founder of a publishing firm called Networlding, we worked side-by-side to inspire and be inspired by one another to write better than we would have written on our own – isolated from this great, collective energy.

To this end, we set and reached our goal of launching the creation of this book in a unified setting of peace, beauty, and strength at the Chicago Yacht Club, a venue close to nature -- the vibrant yet sometimes formidable Lake Michigan, the fifth largest lake in the world, grounded in the center of the United States. By choosing a powerful physical setting to write this book, we started and stayed strong in our individual and collective intent to create and write our stories together.

The impetus and inspiration for the creation of this book? PINKK™.

PINKK™ is the first of its kind empowerment, engagement platform and brand for women and girls. It is about **Powerfully Inspiring Networking and Knowledge with Kindness**. *Hence the acronym that beautifully fits our vision. We do this through women sharing real stories and their journey, with networking, mentoring, coaching and events. Our goal is to provide resources, knowledge and tools to help women succeed by providing a community that welcomes all. We welcome all to become members.*

WHO is this book for? You. All of you who have shown up here and are for some reason holding this book in your hands, looking at this page right now, were meant to learn or share in the stories in it. That connection may come from a phrase, one or more of the stories, or the simple fact that these women have a lot in common with you.

I think we all know a key part of life is simply showing up, being present and wanting to be a part of something bigger than just our self.

In these newly challenging and disruptive times (and even in times of great peace) we can all work together inclusively to better this world dynamic by being of service to one another. In doing so we can help other women (and all) in meaningful ways!

WHY write this and do this now?

Words are powerful. In many religions and faiths, "God" speaks the world into existence. When we affirm ourselves, share ourselves, or communicate with others through powerful words, we can change things for the positive. How we speak about the future helps blaze a path for others to discover and share even greater truths.

So, why *now*? Why *not* now, I ask you? Why we did not do this before is really the question. There is a huge need both locally and globally to help women in all walks of life proactively, and I do not see that need changing. There is more need now for this than perhaps at any other time in the world. Those in "need" come in many shapes and forms. Dignity and respect are paramount.

Getting at the truth/reality is becoming more difficult today as people are often driven by social or corporate agendas, by misinformation, or through miscommunication. Sharing our personal stories of hope and giving hope to others makes the world better. We want a paradigm shift. No small undertaking. I know.

It all must start somewhere, and a grassroots approach is a very good way to start!

So, we begin with this book a series where I have chosen a select group of women who have come forth to create, write, and share their wisdom starting with the power of . . . a single, inspiring word.

The stories shared here have a foundation in kindness. They are about topics like resilience, giving, hunger, passion, positivity and more. With the knowledge that the same challenges we all know exist will continue when good capable women do nothing, these stories break that mold. They are real, raw, and powerful. They're there for you . . . with great love.

It's time to rally, unite and inform. We can use our collective power to create and GIVE. The internet and social media allow for more transparency and for those of us who can hear the beckoning call of a better world . . . to create advocacy groups more readily.

May the words of wisdom offered through a wide variety of unique, compelling stories bring forth ideas that will help you elevate your professional and personal purpose, consciousness and humanity. From this enlightened place may we then work together to empower our future generations of young girls and women. When you expand what you are capable of, everyone around you benefits.

Know that:

> *It's a transformational time for us.*
>
> *We all want to make the world better.*
>
> *Women are at the forefront of change.*
>
> *We are leading the change to purpose.*
>
> *We want to live our authentic personal purpose.*
>
> *Supporting one another is key.*

INTRODUCTION

I'm not one to usually start off with negative news so I've coupled the following facts with a book full of wonderful stories -- antidotes for healing them, maybe not immediately, but, hopefully, sometime in the next decade ☺.

Consider these truths:

Nonprofits focused on women and girls receive just 1.6% of all charitable giving *per the Women's Philanthropy Institute that launched the Women and Girls Index.*

Increasing the funding for women and girl-focused cause groups is a cause of its own. In early October 2019, Melinda Gates pledged to spend over $1 billion over the next decade to help close the gender equality gap. She explained that nonprofits battling women-specific issues are radically underfunded. (They get about $1 for every $5 spent on an arts program or $10 put toward higher education in general). And 90% of that goes toward one cause area: reproductive health. (Source: Fast Company October 7, 2019).

Inequality is still pervasive

46% of the workforce comprised of women, and women account for 51.4% of middle managers in the U.S. but only 4.8% of Fortune 500 CEOs. If not discriminatory and hard to say, by sheer numbers alone, this is inequitable. It certainly isn't a lack of ability. 50% of law school graduates are women, as well as 40% of medical doctors. Even MBA candidates (for decades, nearly an all-male pursuit) are now about 40% female.

We do the same but make less than men

- The female to male earnings ratio in 2016 was 80.5%
- Real median earnings of men are $51,640 and for women is $41,534.
- This makes a huge difference as takes longer to make money, to save money, and we will have to work longer to do so. Lots of reasons for this, I know that. I know many of you have not dealt with this issue and have told me so. To which I toast and say, "That is great! Let's just try to remember it *is* an issue for many." That is all.

Moms have a real challenge

According to research cited in Sheryl Sandberg's book, *Lean In*, 43% of women leave the workforce when they become mothers for an average of two years (this of course varies depending on their position, education, and financial situation). And many of these mothers would rather remain working or return to work sooner, but they can't find employment that will accommodate their needs.

Mothers who choose to remain working are likely to face "the maternal wall," otherwise known as the bias that having children undermines a woman's ability to perform in her career. Mothers are 79% less likely to be hired, half as likely to be promoted, and earn significantly less money than women with comparable resumes who are without children.

This coupled with the fact that there are more of us than men sharing the same issues

The number of females in the US as of October 2, 2019: 168, 225,150 (50.6%). Men as of that same date number 164,021,207 (49.4%).[1]

And women live longer than men and may need to support their families

The approximate ratio by which women over age 85 outnumber men is 2 to 1 (4.2 million to 2.2 million).

But Now, Let's Fly – Destination . . . Kindness!

> "When the moon is in the Seventh House
> And Jupiter aligns with Mars
> Then peace will guide the planets

---

[1] United States of America (USA) Population. Countrymeters.info. Accessed 11-12-19.
https://countrymeters.info/en/United_States_of_America_(USA)

> And love will steer the stars
> This is the dawning of the Age of Aquarius…"

> ~ *Aquarius* from *Hair,* Lyrics by Gerome Ragni;
> James Rado

Written in the late 1960s at the height of the Vietnam War, the song *Aquarius* remains timely today, especially given that we are now actually *living* in the astrological Age of Aquarius. Though astrologers differ in their opinions of exactly when we entered that cycle, the pervading consensus is that it began in the year 2012. Why is this significant concerning kindness, flying by the seat of your skirt and seeing the world through women's eyes, the driving forces behind this book?

The Age of Aquarius is influenced by the best qualities of three factors: Aquarius, Saturn, and Uranus. Predictions about this time in the history of the universe include the shared ideal of spiritual wisdom, global unity in common goals, honesty, peace and kindness move into leadership roles and humanity embraces the concept of all beings receiving care and respect while differences are celebrated. The guiding model of Aquarius is that we all can unite in making the world a better place. The acceleration of the energy of a powerful social conscience blended with visionary intelligence and high regard for revolutionary technologies and progress are innate properties of her sign.

Yes, her. The sign of Aquarius is typically referred to as feminine. The prominence of a divine feminine awakening/renaissance is often associated with this age. The #MeToo movement has shaken things up big time (to put it mildly), paving the way for more equality as we witness separation beginning to fade away. Kindness, compassion, and caring are growing more prominent as the order of the day worldwide. This means greater potential for the possibility of an end to all forms of slavery, the termination of poverty, the combined mindsets of respect, harmony, peace on Earth, and now, the ushering in of what I call "The Age of Kindness."

About the title

Welcome aboard Kindness Airlines! We know you'll enjoy the journey and thank you for joining us as we fly together through this book.

The phrase in this book's title, "Flying by the seat of your pants…" - wait, strike that - "skirts," has its genesis in aviation. Why? In the early days of aircraft, pilots had no sophisticated navigation tools nor the ability to communicate with those the ground. As the phrase caught on in popularity, it has come to mean staying present in the moment, not always being able to plan things out with great certainty, but staying vigilant, agile and creative.

I believe this represents what so many of my female colleagues have experienced through the years—moving from a place of passion and deep intuition women are often attributed to holding along with sprinkles of constant inspiration and, of course, tenacity. This is not about us as women obsessing about obstacles or difficulties that may disrupt our paths. Instead, we stay sharp making smart decisions, but whenever necessary, shifting our trajectories on our life paths as needed.

Take Amelia Mary Earhart, a great example of not only metaphorically flying, but *literally* flying as well. American aviation pioneer and author, Earhart was the first female aviator to fly solo across the Atlantic Ocean. She set many other records, wrote best-selling books about her flying experiences, and was instrumental in the formation of "The Ninety-Nines," an organization for female pilots. She believed that kindness begets kindness.

But Amelia is just one female icon in a rich, long lineage of powerful women whose stories interwoven with kindness, need to be shared. That's *why* this book came to be. The beautiful stories within these pages are offered by a wonderful group of women to give you guidance and inspire ways to tap into the power of kindness every day. Smiling at a stranger as you walk down the street, thanking others when they hold the door open for you, and resolving to do your best to pay the acts of kindness you experience forward—*that's at the heart of flying by the seats of our skirts.*

But unfortunately, kindness is often associated with weakness, manipulation, or fear. The truth is, we cannot truly be kind unless we are truly strong. Kindness is the quality of being friendly, generous, and considerate—all attributes that come from a place of centeredness, emotional, spiritual, and personal strength.

"Unless the teapot is full, you cannot fill another's cup," is the old saying.

When we, as women, come from a place of personal power, knowledge, and wisdom we are naturally kinder, gentler, and more giving.

How do we develop kindness that comes from the heart? By examining our motives. Are we being generous, friendly, considerate and kind in order to manipulate others, or to get something we don't feel justified in asking for? Or do we do it from a place of understanding the power of networking, supporting, and encouraging others?

Becoming a kind person also comes from understanding the power of community, of lending honest help and mentoring, support, and feedback to others. It is not manipulative, but rather pure and authentic. Kindness is love in action. True kindness is a choice. It's not motivated by a desire to manipulate, but by a desire to help. Kindness is the most powerful force in the world. You don't have to be rich, intelligent, powerful or talented to utilize it. You just have to care, to want to change some part of your world or the life of someone in your world. Kindness can be as simple as a smile or taking time to listen compassionately to someone in distress.

There are larger, more structured forms of kindness—like the women across the country who join forces to clean the homes of women undergoing chemotherapy or other severe illnesses. Kindness can be as simple as a meal you prepare for a family grieving the death or loss of a family member. It can mean mentoring at-risk-youth or stepping in to stop a bully. Kindness is powerful because it infuses hope in those who may have run out of hope. Kindness can be setting out a bowl of water outside your business for passersby walking their dogs. Kindness can be handing out bottles of ice-water to strangers working outside on hot days—flagmen, postal workers, joggers, walkers.

Kindness requires no money, talent, or skills, yet often draws on such. Once we understand how kindness works it becomes part of our toolbox in negotiations, relationships, work, business, and in personal interactions. Kindness that comes from strength is not subject to the whims of others. It stands alone in all its humble glory. We are dedicated to the *power* of kindness.

Come along with us as we go flying out into the world with this mission of thoughtfulness and benevolence keeping our spirits airborne. Enjoy the journey through the stories that follow. May you have a wonderful flight and, once again, welcome aboard!

CHARITY
BY MELISSA G WILSON

"Life's most persistent and urgent question is: 'What are you doing for others?'" – Martin Luther King, Jr.

Charity is not a word that most of us use in our daily conversations, but it can significantly hold more weight in our lives if we decide to give it a more contemporary name. Me? I like to think of it as *smart philanthropy.*

Charity makes us feel good. It strengthens our moral and ethical values. It inspires others and, more than anything else, it makes an impact -- on society, on business, on colleagues and customers. When we give by helping others, whether it's our money, time or talent we are making an impact.

But often today it appears that people are less willing to stop to lend a hand when they see others in need. One way we can change our resistance to helping others is to realize that when we take action to help others, we are also helping ourselves. Why?

Take the example of a young man I met while waiting outside a restaurant for a cab one rainy March evening in Chicago. He was a shaggy, red-haired kid huddled up against the outer wall of the restaurant trying to avoid the pelting rain. I overheard his friend call him Jack. I looked over at Jack as he was just about to take his first puff of a cigarette offered to him by his male companion. I don't know what made me walk up to him, but I did. I peered into his blank eyes and said simply, "You know, you would look a lot better without that cigarette in your mouth." With that comment, I turned and stepped away from the two of them as if I didn't care one way or the other if he responded in any way to my suggestion.

I turned my body away from them but did keep an eye on their reaction. To my surprise, Jack, in a rather ceremonial fashion, raised the smoking cigarette he had taken from his friend, held it up high in the misty rain, then dramatically dropped it to the ground and smashed whatever was left of the smoke trailing from its core. At that moment I felt a small thrill in my heart. One charity step forward, many more to follow.

Charity, with its combination of humility mixed with proactive power, makes us realize (if we're willing to examine it) that "there but for the grace of God go I." In other words, giving can humble givers who are will to acknowledge that *we all need help at one time or another*. Charity humanizes us. It makes us better. It connects us.

While most definitions of charity connect its meaning to nonprofit organizations, the traditional definition of charity is "an act or feeling of benevolence, goodwill, or affection." Today, I see charity being used more as an "act" of goodwill toward others. Even deeper, the definition of charity expands as *service to others*. Here, consider the immortal words of Winston Churchill who once said, "...the destiny of mankind is not decided by material computation. When great causes are on the move in the world, we learn we are spirits, not animals, and that something is going on in space and time, which, whether we like it or not, spells duty." Today, I strongly believe it is our duty is to take a long hard look around to see where we can best serve.

Charity in the form of focused service is my passion. It's about making a difference in the world. It's what inspires me. Ten years ago I turned charity and making a difference daily into the mission of my company. By switching my focus of writing my own leadership books to helping others write their leadership books, I found I was able make even more of a difference. It's now been 10 years and, so far, I've been blessed to help more than 120 thought leaders committed to the primary goal of using their brains and brawn to help others through the wisdom that they share in their books. Today I look forward to seeing what the next 10 years will bring.

PINKK ON POINT: Service with the purpose of making a difference is KINDNESS in action. Practice it and it will bring forth more kindness. --
Melissa G Wilson, Founder - Networlding Publishing:
www.networlding.com

WONDER WOMEN
BY MARGARET JOHNSSON

An incredibly nasty divorce left me homeless, penniless, and scared to death. Just ten years prior I had been a successful entrepreneur, having sold my first business to a publicly traded company for over $10 million. And yet, there I was at age 50+ - unable to find a job and losing self-confidence by the minute. Just like being sick with a fever and wondering if I would ever feel normal again, fear was spreading rapidly within me. What if this was my new normal?

Part of the issue was my past success. I hadn't worked for any company, other than businesses I had founded, in over twenty-five years. My prior training as a CPA was outdated by nearly three decades. The majority of my wardrobe and few remaining possessions were locked up in a storage facility. Add to that the facts that I had lost twenty pounds from all the stress and could only afford two meals per day, and what was the end result? I didn't even have proper clothes to go on interviews. I wanted to start another business but had no resources for that. I needed to earn an income immediately. The worst part? I was too embarrassed to reach out to my network for help.

Fortunately, I was about to meet, and reconnect, with some amazing wonder women—all of whom are age 50+. My former office manager, Catherine V., had become a successful realtor and property developer. She used her network to find a charming studio apartment for me. Since I was unemployed, Catherine vouched for me with the landlord's realtor, Sally S. Together these two wonder women convinced the landlord to accept my application, over those of several twenty-year-olds who had also applied (and were employed).

I got a job waitressing so I could at least pay my rent. After a couple of weeks of sleeping on an air mattress the landlord lent me, I saved up enough money to pay the storage facility bill and hire movers to transfer my clothes, bed, desk, and computer into the studio apartment. That then became my headquarters for creating my new life. I thought long and hard about what I could do that would use my entrepreneurial skills in new ways; something where being age 50+ might even be an asset. I landed on two ideas: entrepreneurship education, and strategic business plan development for entrepreneurs.

I tentatively reached out to a few persons from my former professional network. Because the divorce went on for eight years, I had virtually lost contact with everyone. I reached out to Melissa W. She had become a very successful publisher and New York Times best-selling author. I didn't tell her exactly how hard up I was, but I'm pretty sure she could tell. I asked if she knew of anyone that needed a strategic business plan built. She told me she needed such a plan for a new venture she was considering launching and hired me on the spot to start working on it!

This built my confidence, and I approached another female CEO I had been close with, Sarah, McC. She also hired me to work on a plan for a new business she had already launched but wanted to grow it rapidly. Having gained the faith (and grace) of these two wonder women to work on their business plans, I considered this the official launch of a sole-practitioner consulting firm.

These strategic business planning projects didn't provide enough income to quit waitressing, but boosted my confidence, inspiring me to approach higher education organizations to see if I could teach entrepreneurship classes. That's when the first of several new wonder women entered my life. The president of an association for entrepreneurship education, Dr. Rebecca C., accepted my proposal to teach an entrepreneurship workshop at the association's annual conference, and agreed to a revenue-sharing arrangement. (I found out later that revenue-sharing arrangements were not the norm; that most conference presenters work free-of-charge.)

I was excited because several persons registered for the workshop. However, I would not get paid until after the workshop's completion. I didn't have enough money to purchase the plane ticket to get to the conference. I reached out to a very successful woman CEO I had known several years prior. I didn't know how to ask her, but finally told her my story over lunch. Even though she hadn't seen me in years, Jeanne G. gave me $1,500 to get to the conference. And then, after the conference, she wouldn't take the money back. She told me to pay it forward to help someone else in need!

The workshop was well-received. I used the post-workshop survey feedback to approach another new wonder woman, Dr. Claudia S. She is a pioneer in online education and is dean of the college of business at a university about one mile from my studio apartment/corporate headquarters. Even though it was mid-semester, Dr. Claudia S. listened to my story and hired me to teach management, strategy, and entrepreneurship to MBA students. She also gave me a consulting assignment to help launch a center for innovation and entrepreneurship for the university. There was only one catch—we had zero budget. We submitted our first grant application within one month. We did not get it. We applied for a second grant a month later. This time we DID get it! We were the only grantee in the state of Illinois awarded a national grant from the AARP Foundation (whose mission is eliminating senior poverty).

I have now spent the last two-and-a-half years leading the AARP Foundation's Work For Yourself @50+ program for the state of Illinois. Through this grant I have had the amazing blessing to work with over 200 persons interested in starting on the path to entrepreneurship. Over 70% of the participants in the program are women age 50+, creating new lives for themselves and making the world a better place through the ventures they are launching. It is my honor and pleasure to be surrounded by so many wonder women, including all of those featured in this wonderful book. Thank you, Athena and PINKK, for the opportunity to tell my story. I hope it encourages others to reach out for help and/or to help those in need. And I am happy to help any and all that contact me in search of an entrepreneurial guide.

Please connect with me at:

https://www.linkedin.com/in/marge-johnsson-8a57404/

PINKK on POINT: Kindness is compassion and supporting one another at all phases of our lives and sharing our journeys.

EVOLVE
BY ERIN COUPE

We all grow, change, and hopefully evolve throughout our lives. As babies we go from lying on our backs, helpless and dependent, to rolling over, crawling, walking, and running. Since the core meaning of evolution is the gradual development of something growing more complex, that means we can evolve through the choices we make and the intentions we set for ourselves. Evolving means changing ourselves for the better. Some people seek out a life coach, therapist, or mentor who can guide them through their evolution process. Others attend workshops, read, or share their journey with friends. The process or path we take is different for us all, but no matter what path we choose, evolution involves looking at one's own beliefs, self, personality, actions, and choices.

EVOLVE

In my twenties, I worked on Wall Street in a competitive, male-dominated and cutthroat environment. During these impressionable years early in my career, I saw a lot of oppressive behavior and outright unprofessional, unfair treatment of others. I am grateful for the innate knowing that I was not a victim of what surrounded me or what I witnessed. Instead, I took it upon myself to be a positive light in the dark rooms. I commanded positive conversation and approached people with an upbeat attitude even though the easy route would have been the path of bitterness.

See, I could have taken on the negativity around me and treated others the way that I was treated. After all, the culture was attempting to teach me I was only as worthy or as good as my boss told me I was; to promote the illusion that managers were the ones to decide my future. But my interpretation was quite the opposite. I could see and *feel* that what was coming at me was just a projection of these managers' own insecurity and pain. Unfortunately, most of my managers during this time were women, always older and more senior than me. They believed it was their right to pass onto me the ill treatment that they received on their road to management.

The interrogation and passive-aggressive behaviors were a lot to handle, and that produced anxiety and undue stress in my professional life. I stuck this out for several years and when I finally made the conscious decision to leave Wall Street, I swore to myself that I would not work for another woman. I believed women in business who were older than me would not be supporters of younger women.

My next role was a pivotal moment in my career. I completely changed directions professionally. I had built incredible business skills while on Wall Street and possessed soft skills transferable to various fields. After soul searching, I knew that architecture was a passion of mine. I love design, grandiosity and urban environments, and the energy of a city like Chicago revved me up. Before resigning from Wall Street at 30 years old, I networked like crazy with people in the architecture community.

That's when I met Gina. Gina was about one year older than me and had been in architecture most of her career. She was being recognized within her firm and quickly was moving into a leadership position. Thrilled to know her, when we met for coffee or a glass of wine over the course of six months, I grew enamored of the confidence, poise and contentment in her spirit. She was someone I deeply respected, and I wanted to be around more.

As Gina and I got to know each other and our relationship grew deeper over several meetings, we knew we wanted to work together. However, I had zero background in architecture, so in what capacity could we do this? It was Gina that challenged me to reflect and think about my strengths. As I thought about it, I landed on the fact that building relationships and doing business were things I was very good at and enjoyed. So, as I expressed this, she suggested that I do business development for her firm. I had never done business development, nor worked in architecture. It was uncharted territory. But rather than being fearful, I was ecstatic. I couldn't say yes fast enough.

This was a first for me to experience a real relationship with a woman in leadership—someone who was kind, compassionate and empathetic. It was Gina that transformed my view toward working with women. She showed me what true leadership is, and she led from the heart. Not easily deterred, she treated everyone pretty much the same. She ultimately showed me the way to believing in myself and my abilities.

The success that she and I saw in that business over the next several years was immense, as was my own personal growth. That pivotal relationship with Gina came at a time in my life that was so meaningful and appropriate.

Always Be Evolving! Personal evolution is not something that is always tangible. Most often it happens right in front of our eyes, yet we only see it in hindsight. The universe presents opportunities, experiences (good and bad) and circumstances for us to evolve. Sometimes all it takes is one person, one relationship to send you down a path you least expected. Take the turn, listen to the words, walk the yellow brick road and see what lies ahead. It is meant for you and is waiting to teach you something. You then get the chance to carry that forward and help the next person evolve.

Reflect. If you want to evolve, take time every day, or at least once a week to sit and reflect about things happening in your life. You can do this as you have your morning coffee or tea, or breakfast. Instead of checking email or text messages, set aside 5-15 minutes to think back on the day before. What did you do differently? How did you approach a problem or challenge? Was it better or more mature and evolved, or not? What do you want to do differently today? Maybe you're dealing with some mean girls or bullies at work. Maybe you have a problem with listening or being calm. What do you need to do to improve in those areas?

Self-improvement. Another word for Evolving is Self-Improvement. Self-improvement can mean anything from reading a self-help book on a specific quality you want to master, to seeing a therapist to create a grand plan of self-improvement in areas you don't feel ready or able to change alone. Successful, happy women are always improving something about themselves. It can be anything from their networking skills, listening skills, financial management, style and wardrobe, to writing skills. It's up to you. There's no race and no certificate to aim for—only a decision to improve the things in your life that you feel the need to improve.

Erin Coupe, Vice President

CBRE | Advisory & Transaction Services | Occupier

PINKK on POINT: Evolving. Just like service, it's up to you. Do it for you and you will *inspire* kindness in others.

BRAVE
BY T.E.W.

On September 11, 2018, I was sitting in the Minneapolis airport waiting on my flight back to Chicago. Like most millennials, I was browsing on Instagram. I decided to check out my favorite Minnesotan's Instagram page and came across a post from Need Voices for stories about suicide. I realized I had actually never written my story or truly told it in its entirety. Given it was a day of remembrance and reflection, I figured I'd take a go at it. At a minimum, it's always cathartic to get your thoughts out and maybe it will do more by helping others. So here goes...

It was a Tuesday afternoon, and I was napping after high school volleyball practice. My dad called me, and I remember answering, half awake. I said, "Dad, I'm tired. Can we talk later?" He replied, "Sure, I love you." And I hung up. It was the last time I spoke to my dad and last time he spoke with anyone. Later that night, he took his own life.

I remember the following day my mom came into my room after school. She was on the phone, crying. Alarmed, I asked, "What's wrong?" She could barely mutter the words, "I'm talking to your grandfather..." I immediately asked if it was Gran Gran, my 90-year-old great grandmother. Her response was one that would forever change the course of my life. She said, sobbing, "No, no, it's your father, he killed himself..."

Everything went black and quiet. I remember feeling sick to my stomach and confused—in complete shock and disbelief. I mean, didn't I just speak to him yesterday? Wasn't he supposed to travel in for my volleyball game later that week? My parents were divorced. We had recently moved from my hometown and he was living in another city, about an hour away, but he still made every effort to come to my games and cheer me on. I couldn't understand...I could not comprehend what my mom just told me.

The next few days were a haze. I remember going to school the next morning with my mother and speaking to each of my teachers to get a pass from class and my homework. I stood silently as she told them one by one that my father just passed away and that I would be out for a while. I saw my friends and told them he passed away but never stated the reason. It was 1999, and I was 15 years old. Death by suicide was NOT discussed.

Later that week, we drove down to my hometown for the viewing and funeral services. I remember seeing my grandparents, the sweetest souls on this planet. There was absolute devastation in their eyes. Seeing my grandfather break down in tears shattered my already broken heart. I remember sobbing and seeing my three best friends and their moms.

I remember the viewing. It was an open casket; he looked so peaceful and handsome. I convinced myself he must have had a reason... I mean, there had to be a reason. There had to be a logical reason that a father of four, with a successful law practice, not to mention an intelligence I've yet to encounter again, and the most charismatic personality I've ever seen, took his own life. He must have been hurting; depressed, desperate, saw no other way. There just had to be a reason that made sense.

I decided right then and there that I would accept his decision. Was it really a choice? I wouldn't be a victim. That is not what he would have wanted, and I promised to make him proud and be strong for myself and my family. No more tears, except alone in my room listening to our favorite tunes. Aaron Neville gets me every time.

They held the funeral at a church, but it was important that we made it a celebration of his life—full of love, music, and memories. I am positive that was the first time Garth Brooks was played in that church! I know that he was smiling down during that song. We also played the hymn "It Is Well with My Soul," which is next to "Amazing Grace" in the United Methodist Hymnal. We all believed that all was now well with his soul.

Looking back, I can't believe I only missed three days of school, made straight A's in all honors classes and went on about my life. Isn't that what he would have wanted? He never let me make excuses for being anything less than excellent before and always had the bar set very high. I had to continue to make him proud!

Of course, back at school there were lots of questions and people didn't know how to react. No one I knew had experienced an immediate family member's death. I told everyone he had a heart attack. That was believable, right? Thankfully, we had recently moved to a new city. No one there had read the newspaper from my hometown; the one that thoughtlessly published an article about what really happened. It was 1999—before Google, Facebook, Twitter, etc., and my story stuck.

I went on to attend the University of Florida, which was his law school Alma Mater. My family always said he would be so proud, smiling down from heaven. Yes, as Methodists we believed he still went to heaven, or at least my very religious grandparents convinced us that was true. They had to believe that his soul lived on to cope with the devastation of losing their only son. While they turned to God and their faith, I turned to my friends, boys, partying (somewhat responsibly), and escaping. But I kept on chugging along, no pun intended.

When I was 19, I finally confided in two girlfriends about what really happened. I told them that my father was the smartest man I knew; literally, a brilliant mind. But when it came to women and alcohol, he failed miserably. He couldn't set boundaries and struggled with depression. He had the biggest heart but couldn't say no to his temptations or demons. He left my mom for another woman and later married her. While I didn't like her, he seemed happy at first, and they had two kids together.

Most of my memories of him were of happy times, full of family, fun and laughter. However, there are some not so pleasant memories that stand out, too. Times when he was in despair, visibly hurting, filled with shame, beaten down. Even at 11 and 14 years of age, I could see him hurting. Nevertheless, he was a dedicated father. Never in a million years could I imagine his decision to end his life and leave a 15, 12, 3- and 2-year-old fatherless. Didn't he know we needed him? Didn't he know we idolized him? Didn't he know we loved him unconditionally?!?

What I've learned over time is none of that mattered. I was too young at the time to know all the details of why he did it, but I later found out he had recently divorced his second wife, was struggling financially and potentially could lose his law license. I guess he thought providing financial security via life insurance was a better option than for him to continue living. Or maybe he couldn't face the shame of another failed marriage, the fact that he had a drinking problem, or asking my grandparents for more money. He was the prodigal son, after all. Maybe it was his clinical depression that he was incredibly skillful at masking. He was in therapy, seeing our pastor regularly and seemed so happy. I would give back everything I owned to have him back. I didn't need anything but his love, support, and that infectious smile.

Over the years, I've learned to accept I'll never really know the real reason, and almost 20 years later, I'm finally at peace with that. I've had my share of ups and downs with his death and his decision to end his life. I often think about how sad and scared he must have been, how lonely and desperate he was when he went into the guest bathtub of my grandparent's condo, wearing only Umbro gym shorts and pulled the trigger. I imagine tears falling down his face while he sat there thinking this was the only way out, and the best thing for his family. Even in death, he always put others first. That image crushes me. It literally makes it hard to breathe.

I always think back to that Tuesday afternoon when he called me, the last person he spoke with, and I hung up before saying, "I love you, too." Could those four little words have saved him? I'll never know.

What I do know is, while I lied about the cause of his death for a long time, over the years I've heard about other people who have lost loved ones to suicide. Unfortunately, it hit too close to home when my best friend lost her 30-year-old brother to suicide. I was there for her like no one else could be because of our shared tragedy. It's a devastating experience that binds you unspeakably. You don't have to use words, you just understand.

Over time, I was finally brave enough to share his story with others. I got to a space where I could tell people about my dad and the amazing man he was. I no longer harbored embarrassment, guilt and shame when sharing how he actually died. I know who he was and what he stood for. Most importantly, I know that he loved his family. I have learned to accept that he was in pain and made a decision that he thought was best.

A silver lining from experiencing grief at such a young age is that I've been able to help others who have lost loved ones to process their grief. I've also been able to help those who have lost loved ones to suicide own their story and work through the guilt and shame associated with it. There is power in knowing that you aren't alone; sharing your story and just being there to listen.

Each time I read that someone passed unexpectedly with no reason listed, especially younger people, suicide is the first thought to cross my mind. My heart breaks for their loved ones, knowing what they are about to go through. It's a devastating, tragic and gut-wrenching feeling. If I could share words with them, I would say, "You will survive this. You are strong, you are brave, you will move forward. You will hurt, you will grieve, you will hear a song that brings you to your knees sobbing. You will need to rely on others, you'll learn you aren't alone, you will try to live each day to the fullest. You will live for them and share your story, grief and pain."

For you lucky souls who never have to experience this, you can help, too. You can listen to others, you can avoid judgement, you can seek to understand. You can be kind; you can let others know they are not alone. You can choose to live and most importantly—you can choose to love.

How to Be Brave

Bravery is an acquired skill. Some people embrace being brave and others reject it. Bravery forces some of us to dig deep to find the courage to get through an unexpected event, while others get a chance to build up those skills a few moments a day.

The good news is bravery can be developed. Pushing yourself out of your comfort zone each day allows you to build bravery over time. Bravery doesn't mean you have to jump out of an airplane or swim with sharks. Bravery is built while taking chances and risks, doing new things, vocalizing your feelings, saying "No," where you've always said "Yes," in the past.

Being brave can mean examining the aspects of yourself you don't like. It can mean having that difficult conversation with someone, being vulnerable, reflecting on our shortcomings, learning a new skill, going back to college, or leaving a bad relationship. Sometimes we need to be brave for others—a friend, child, spouse, or other family member. It is important to remember that the braver you become, the more possibilities and opportunities you open yourself up to receive.

You Can Be Brave

Practice being brave 10-20 seconds a day. It might be as simple as wearing something you've never worn for fear of what others might say.

No one is brave all at once. You may have experienced something largely traumatic, like a death, an illness, a loss. At times, you may have to braver than you feel capable of being. Just remember to take one small step at a time and ask for help when you feel scared or uncertain. You don't have to be brave all the time. There will be times when you are brave for others and when others are brave for you. We're all in this together.

Learn to be vulnerable. Being vulnerable can be scary. There are ways for you to be vulnerable without sharing vulnerable emotions. You can ask for help, admit when you made a mistake, or share an imperfect idea. It is okay to start small. When you are more comfortable being vulnerable, challenge yourself to think of safe relationships where you can share more of your doubts, concerns, or fears. It's okay to need others and turn to others at certain times. Learn when it's appropriate and beneficial to do so.

Reflect on your own shortcomings and strengths. While it sometimes can be scary to look at our own shortcomings and failures, it can be even more intimidating to reflect on our strengths because it makes you vulnerable to criticism and judgment.

Embrace failure, don't avoid it. Most of us were raised to avoid fear and hide our failures. The truth is, we learn and grow the most from our failures. Remember to embrace your failures, examine them, and most importantly, learn from them.

PINKK on POINT: Brave is saying I love you. Do that and spread kindness.

AWAKENING
BY ANGIE COMINOS KOEHLER

*"You learn who you are by unlearning who
they taught you to be."*
~ *Nikki Rowe*

Yoga saved me. It's why I'm currently teaching yoga and delivering workshops on Mindfulness at my studio and at DePaul. I am also writing meditations that I use in my workshops. In October 2019, I launched a career coaching business marketing to college graduates and young professionals through universities. I have two beautiful and strong sons that are my pride and joy; they have always had my heart and always will. If it sounds like a wonderful and peaceful life, that's because it is. But it didn't spring fully formed and perfect like magic. Happiness is a process—one we often arrive at only after much struggle and personal pain. Rose bushes have thorns for a reason—to remind us beauty and a healing fragrance come at a price.

My journey began a decade ago. I felt I had lost the power to make choices in my life due to commitments I made. I found myself repeating patterns of enabling behavior to those in my path, which was depleting to me and disempowering to those lives I affected. I believed that by providing enough direction, control, insight and wisdom,

I would actually change another person; how they thought, behaved and existed in the world. I felt responsible for everything and everyone. I felt that the weight of the entire world was on my shoulders. I was tired, angry, and resentful. Disappointment was my go-to feeling for comfort. It was a thick, dark security—a warm, cozy emotional blanket that kept me safe.

I thought the power for me to attain joy in my life was in someone else's hands, so I patiently waited for the change I longed for to occur. But while I was waiting, I eventually was let go from a 32-year career in training, development and coaching people with a great company that I really enjoyed. This turned my world upside down, and for a while I wondered if my disappointment blanket would be large enough to cover me.

I had always worked hard enough to do anything I wanted in life. I paid my own way through college. I solved issues on my own. I moved to a new city on my own. I also started a new career on my own without a second thought or doubt. I was not a victim. I considered myself very self-sufficient and independent. What I didn't know at the time, though, seems crystal clear to me now. But I could not understand it until I experienced it for myself—the only way around is through.

Only by looking from the present backward could I see, feel, understand, and then finally own *t*he truth that I was responsible for all of my actions. Additionally, I can't change anyone else, especially if they have no desire to change themselves. In my situation, I thought if I tried hard enough and long enough, positive change would come. I just needed to be more patient. I was relentless. I would not quit. I creatively kept trying to come up with new ideas, action plans and due dates that would move me closer to the outcomes I wanted to see happen in my life. I felt like a hamster on a wheel, working harder and harder, but in reality, never moving forward. I just kept ending up right back where I started. Something had to change. And finally... it did.

Yoga

I attended my first hot yoga class when the studio offered a week of free, unlimited yoga. I cannot say it was love at first sight, as I needed to be much better hydrated to go the distance. I also had no clue how to form the poses being taught—not unusual, but it bothered me. Because it still intrigued me, I stuck in there. I went back to a second class with a different teacher.

After the second class, that teacher, who I now refer to as my soul sister, said to me, "You are gripping in fear." I had no clue what she meant and no idea how these words would change me and my path forever. I wondered; *How could she know that?* I asked her what she meant, and she shared that she could see the tightness in my body as I moved. Well, I kept going to her class, more out of defiance than anything else.

As I kept going, something started to change in me. I became stronger and softer. My heart was opening slowly, and simultaneously, my mind started shifting to show me I was in charge of my choices, no one else. I started realizing I could create the life I wanted along with the feelings I longed to experience on my own without waiting passively for someone to do what I needed them to do.

I also realized that there were other paths available to me. I found those times spent at yoga class sacred and reflective, empowering, and healing at the same time. I soon became a regular, wanting and needing the spiritual strength that yoga provided me, along with the physical strength I was developing. For the first time in my life, I put my wants and needs ahead of anyone else. Initially, this act of extreme self-care felt foreign, selfish, and wrong. But over time and with a lot of practice, I'm now able to continue to make choices in my life that are good for me, first. As an added bonus, I have found this also ends up being better for those with whom I interact. My yoga practice literally shifted my thinking and then my world.

So, this is what I know to be true: Once we awaken, we cannot turn back. This is the path to becoming stronger than you ever thought you could be. I chose the path that was best for me. A friend shared with me the analogy that choosing yourself is like seeing someone else drowning who won't relax enough for you to help them. Instead, they pull you down with them. At that point, you have the choice to keep trying to save them and drown with them or save yourself. In my case, I chose to save me.

Five years later, today I have a new marriage, a new career, and am a yoga teacher myself, delivering inspirational, thoughtful messages to my students along with mindfulness workshops. Like I said, yoga saved me. I hope that I can now inspire others to realize that choices and paths exist for them they may not yet know exist. If they keep showing up and doing the mind/body/spiritual work of yoga, they will experience the magic of yoga and peel back the layers to discover their brave, true selves— the person they yearn to be. As a result, there will be no end to their continual state of becoming all they can be.

I am no longer afraid of change, the unknown or times of gray. But I am open to becoming, helping others and enjoying the journey with an open heart, mind, and body. My goal now is to help others uncover possibilities they never thought existed, one step at a time through yoga and career coaching.

I have learned to channel my need to control outcomes and, instead, let go with loving kindness. I daily send positive energy and thoughts to those that make choices to stay stuck and not move forward. I hope that they someday find the strength within themselves to come out from their protective shell and discover what a big beautiful life is available to them.

ANGIECOMINOS@ yahoo.com

PINKK on POINT: Let anger go and kindness will prevail.

HONORED
BY SUSAN DVORA

Travel Journal: South Africa, 2004

Words are inadequate to describe today, but I will try.

Sunday services at Father Masengo's Church and Centre, Isipingo, Kwa Zulu Natal

I am picked up at a flat by a driver sent by Bishop Mtetwah. My friend Phumapi joins us and tells me I must cover my head in church to show respect. I don't have a scarf, so I grab a piece of fabric from my quilting workshop materials and fashion a headpiece which pleases them. The driver, a young man in his thirties, flirts with me and tells me he will consider me for a second wife. I ask him to explain the second wife concept in his culture. He tells me it comes from man's need when the first wife has her monthly period. During that time, she is not to be with her husband or cook for him or serve him, so he takes a second wife for those times. We tease about equality of the sexes and talk about male chauvinism. By the time we arrive at church, we are dear friends.

I am escorted to a small building described as the church's home for visiting church officials. I am told that the Bishop arrived at four in the morning from Leshoto, where he was helping to facilitate the church general assembly. He is pleased I've returned for services. An elder of the church, Nonhlanhla has been assigned to be my escort and translator. She is a tall, stately woman who tells me about her trip to Washington D.C. in the nineties and her enjoyment of that trip. We then stand outside the chapel, waiting for the next hymn to begin. That will be our signal that it is an appropriate time for us to enter.

Soon it's time. Phumapi tells me to follow Nonhlanhla as I am a VIP. Phumapi goes to the back of the church. I'm escorted to the pulpit and seated with other women elders next to the speaker's podium. I look out on approximately 500 or more people. The men on one side are all neatly dressed in jackets and ties, and some wear white robes. Behind them are some of the 300 people who live on the property—most are survivors of indescribable traumatic life experiences during the struggle. On the other side, rows and rows of women are all dressed in uniform—blue skirts and sashes, white headpieces and jackets or white robes. Surrounding me, the older women wear the same uniforms but somehow look more regal, more important.

There are no organs or instruments, yet there is a kind of music generated by an amazing clapping of the hands during the singing. This first melody is haunting as are those to follow, and every bit as moving as any synagogue or church music I've ever heard.

There is a kind of responsive reading of scripture. I notice a few tattered Bibles shared throughout the audience. Zulu and Lusutu are the languages of this Apostle Church.

People stand, kneel, and sit throughout the next hour of the service, and then the Bishop comes to the podium. Nonhlanhla is translating but I can't seem to make out her whispers. I soon realize that the Bishop is introducing me. He makes eye contact with me, greets me with a wide genuine smile, and everyone stands and applauds me.

I sit while taking in the attention and then rise to acknowledge this sweet welcome. He realizes that I'm unable to understand what's being said, so he appoints a male translator and he speaks more slowly. I can't remember his words, but they consider him a prophet and a healer. He's speaking about his wonderment in meeting me and his great desire to go to America. He reminisces about his trip to England years ago and what it meant to him. He certainly let me know that my visit is quite extraordinary for his people, and he is most proud to have me there.

There is some whispering, and I feel something is being organized. I learn that the audience is being told I can't stay until four when the brass band usually plays, so the Bishop changed the service. He shortened it by an hour and sent out a message it was time for the band. More singing, more clapping… more spirit in that space than you can imagine. I'm touched by the order and discipline and respect. This Bishop is a gifted leader who tries with every word and deed to bring dignity and hope to his people.

Throughout the service, I noticed African scenes through the small windows… women carrying large items on their heads walking near the property. Small children marching near the nursery school building using pieces of cardboard as instruments. Suddenly new images appear... men with uniforms and white gloves carrying shiny silver horns and large drums. I hear the sounds of a band coming closer and closer to the church. The sounds become louder. The back doors of the church opened for an amazing procession.

First come the elders marching proudly, then two men with walking sticks, then the bandleader with his tall decorated baton. A sea of blue and white movement with loud music so repetitive that it felt like it was getting louder and louder on your behalf to put you in touch with your soul and your G-d. The procession was all about precision and persistence and pride. There were 30 horn players (trumpets, French horns, trombones, etc.) right in front of me; circling, marching, moving in a haunting and uplifting movement. I smile, suddenly realizing that the Bishop is in the circle, playing a horn as well. His personal movement, melody and grace were the example others were following.

When the band entered, we stood, and we remained on our feet for the next hour of this incredible performance. I was moved to tears I could not control... tears expressing my feeling of privilege to be present for this weekly ritual being performed with even more spirit on my behalf. I have often been the only white person at a particular site but being the only white person here and the only American to experience this was too much. Who do you tell?

How do you tell? It feels important to tell! And then the day became even more special...

Nonhlanha began motioning me to follow her. Through marching and swaying, we became two of five women leading the march down the center aisle. I quickly picked up the cadence and the movement. A precise matching step, the swinging of the right arm high in the front, then back by your side and forward again. As we went down the aisle, people started to wave to me, so I waved back with my left hand. We exited the back of the church behind the band, still playing powerfully to the Lord on this sunny day in these bare surroundings. There were more of the 300 people who live there lined up to watch. They wave to me; so again, I wave back.

I now know how the Pope and Mother Teresa felt when they were honored in similar ways. We marched and swayed to the end of that road, turned and marched to the end of the next one. They guided us into precision turns, and I felt so included...so much a part of the congregation. After perhaps another half hour, I was pulled from the procession and escorted back to a central building. Knowing my time was now limited, the women elders wanted to serve me juice and cookies before my journey 'home.' We introduced ourselves, and Nonhlanhla promised to keep in touch. The driver's mother was there. Her husband came by and teased that he wanted me for a second wife, just like his son. I realized that was a sort of compliment to me. They thought my headpiece was stunning, and they were honored by my presence.

If you ever want to feel humbled, uplifted and in touch with your Creator in a whole new way; if you ever want to be inspired, honored, and feel as important as a President or Pope, I suggest you attend Sunday services at the Father Marengo Church in Isipingo, Kwa Zulu Natal, South Africa!

Note: With the help of friends, I was able to help Bishop Mtetwah attend a Minister's conference in Atlanta, Georgia a month after this service. He met with major leaders in the American civil rights movement and participated with clergy from all over the country. He includes memories of his trip in many of his services and the trip continues to inspire his work.

suedvora@gmail.com

PINKK on POINT: Kindness is everywhere. When you believe and march side by side the kindness marches on after you are gone.

DAUGHTERS
BY MARILYN DAWSON

Your family is one of the most important influences on your life. The joys, challenges and support we experience as children have an enormous impact on our lives, far into adulthood.

Most parents do all that they can to support and nurture their children and to provide them with best life that they can. Each generation seeks to recreate the positive aspects of their childhoods and learn from or improve upon whatever difficulty or psychological challenges they may have experienced.

Our sons and daughters often illuminate our own strengths and weaknesses. We share our journeys with them and learn from the children that came before us. I share mine with my daughters.

My mom got married very young to escape an unhappy home. She was the oldest of six children, five daughters and one son. She left nursing school, married my dad, and had four children by the time she was 29. She left the marriage because my father was an alcoholic and had other issues, in a time before mandated child support. She joined support groups, got counseling, and worked multiple jobs to support the family. It took a lot of courage and it was a shaky, stressful time. She did everything she could with the resources she had.

While working those jobs, she went to the local community college and got an associate degree. Our local paper published a feature about "the working mother of four who was also in school." In time, she worked her way up in a large global corporation and became a successful regional sales manager. She won sales trips, traveled, built a home, and achieved things she never would have dreamed of as a young single mother.

My childhood influenced me in multiple ways, some positive and some that were not. As the oldest, I was very responsible at a young age, helping to take care of my siblings and helping my mom. Mom raised us to be self-sufficient. We were often on our own; there were money stresses and life stresses, and some trauma. We worked through it, supporting each other and our mom, as best we could.

Growing up, I observed life in times of change. I saw how perseverance can take you through a variety of challenges—emotional, physical, financial, and personal. My mom demonstrated all of those. I also observed her helping others through difficult times, even with the very little she had herself. That definitely had an impact. She not only gave encouragement, she also sought help and support, both of which are such meaningful life skills. Looking back at my mom's coping skills made me think more about my own life and what shaped it.

I am a list-maker and goal-setter. I often use the word *tenacious* to describe myself. It's especially important in my work. That ability to stay the course, flex, find options, and make things happen has had rewards. Watching my mom set goals and achieve them definitely influenced me.

Influences from my childhood motivated me to create a different, more stable family life than the one I lived. I have two *daughters* and they are my greatest joy. I've had some terrific *experiences* and relationships in my work, yet I feel that my most meaningful accomplishment is that I've been able to provide a very different life for my daughters than I had. I think children who grow up with stability and a wide network of support and love carry that with them into life. Wanting this for my children gave me clarity in how I wanted to live, partner and parent, and how I wanted to take part in their lives. Seeing life through their experiences, being a part of their world, being able to encourage, support, and guide them has been so rich. It's immeasurable.

When I was a child, we moved often. While there were supportive, helpful friends, we lacked a consistent network, and we were not that connected to the community. My mother was always working or in school and was extremely pressed for time. She was still evolving as a young mother. She had few resources and enormous responsibility. There was no one with whom to share the burden of raising four children. She didn't have the opportunities or support I've had.

My daughters have enjoyed the support and involvement of so many adults—our community of friends, other parents and family—adults who gladly provided coaching, volunteering, leading, and support to those who needed it.

There is no perfect life, it's full of joy, challenges, and learning. There are so many factors that influence us or cause a change in direction. We've been fortunate to have been a part of a caring community with a network of supportive friends and neighbors. That phrase, "it takes a village" is so true. When other parents become like an extended family, that is a gift.

Now my daughters are in their twenties and are creating their own lives. It's so good to see them thriving and making their own ways. It's so rewarding to see how they have created their own communities and how they care for others. Their hearts are big. They are so empathic, and they want to make the world a better place. I look forward to seeing what's next for them, as I'm also thinking about what's next in my life.

I've been thinking about the ways you learn from your parents, both the strong, positive lessons, and the lessons that come in other ways; lessons that influence how you want to want to shape your life differently. That is also a strong legacy. No doubt my daughters will have both kinds of lessons from their own childhood.

mdawson112@gmail.com

PINKK on POINT: A village and community created on kindness will prevail for the next generation. Let's do that.

GODWINK
BY DIANA PREVIS

C all it synchronicity or coincidence, fate, destiny, a sign from God or happenstance, things happen to all of us for a reason. Some grab our attention; others slip by us with no awareness on our part. But sometimes things happen that bring us up short in our steps. Some people, like author Squire Rushnell, call those amazing, out-of-the-blue events "Godwinks"—seemingly miraculous, unfathomable coincidences that stop us in our tracks and make us question why they happened. Rushnell coined the word "Godwinks" to describe the little "coincidences" that don't feel like a coincidence but seem to be a tangible connection to a divine source. Signs, small or large, appear in our lives to confirm a suspicion, to send a message, or tell us we're doing something wrong or right. Diana Previs recounts her own Godwink—a sign from God she was on the right path.

A Sign from God: Diana Previs

If you ever look in your life for signs confirming you are doing the right thing and can't find them, just ask. If there is anything that I would want to teach someone or those who come after me, I would say learning to communicate with the Universe. By doing so, you will find out at least these two things: 1) You are never alone, and 2) You are loved. I have experienced many of these moments, but for today, I will share with you a sign from God that I was definitely on the right path. It begins with what I call "the journey." I was living in California when I received a call to come back home to help my father and brother as my dad was preparing to go into hospice care. I didn't have a relationship with him really, so was hoping in those last few days or hours we could make up for lost time.

The most important mission for me was to be with him in his final moments and be able to help his transition to the other side. My biggest fear, since he had a near-death experience three years previously, was that he would die alone, and that my brother would be the one to find him. It was a likely scenario because my dad lived by himself and my brother checked on him daily. I wanted to do anything I could to protect my brother from that lonely, harsh discovery.

Bill (my Dad) had emotionally checked out years before; for all points and purposes he had already died of a broken heart from the loss of his wife, his girlfriend, and his daughter. He was a walking shell of a man. When I finally got my dream chance to move to California, I took it. However, I would communicate with my dad by having telepathic conversations with him daily as I walked the beach.

I inspired him from afar to let go. If you let go, you let God in. I believe we are usually given some time to prepare for this major event—before we leave this world and go onto the next. You must be completely at peace with the significant people in your life. I had no idea whether I was successful in spiritually communicating with him from 2,000 miles away. Then I got my brother's call telling me it was time to come home. My dad, slowly dying of old age among other maladies, was ready to go into hospice care.

I quickly jumped on a plane filled with one big trepidation. I did not know what I would face back home. I had no clue I was about to manifest the biggest wish I ever had. Actually, two wishes—to have an amazing relationship with the first man in my life, and then to be with him in his final moments. That is a co-creative experience of the highest order. So, here is what happened next. For the next 30 days I spent time with him, close by while they transferred him from the hospital to a private hospice center, which resembled a ski lodge more than a care facility.

We shared many funny moments together, and a few touching memories that came up while talking about his life. He was always a man of few words, and sometimes not kind ones. His cantankerous nature could drive anyone out of the room faster than anything. However, when he was sweet, and you felt like you had done something that pleased him, there was nowhere else you wanted to be. I spent every day with him and started journaling my thoughts towards the end of those 30 days. I started writing to him in my journal. I now believe he heard me energetically. A spiritual coach informed me five days before his passing that I was the reason he had not passed yet, that he felt that I was not ready for him to go. I told her that was absolutely ridiculous.

I mean, after all, I had stopped everything in my life to come home for this big event. Of course, I was ready! Are we ever ready? In truth, I wasn't… so that very day I started to have conversations with him in my mind, about how I was getting myself ready. We shared our last dinner together that night. We had a normal conversation, and as I prepared myself mentally, I shared with him telepathically about letting go. The next day he started his descent, slowly sleeping more and more each day. I realized as I witnessed this that he would let me be by his side at his final passing. My wish three years before of being with him at the end was about to manifest. I somehow knew it would happen at night or in the dark, and I wanted to be there.

I brought my clothes and stayed there in his room that Friday night. In the middle of the night, he tried to leave, but I was not ready. I did some energy work on his feet, and he rebounded. The nurse, Joan, (also my mother's name—coincidence? I don't think so) came in at 3:00 am. She tried to comfort him, but he refused any morphine. In the middle of the night, I fed him a honeydew melon, and he fell back to sleep. The next 24 hours were actually comical. He would wake up out of nowhere and ask me random things, like was I ever going to make any money from my startup venture? My brother assured him I would marry some rich old guy, so he didn't need to worry.

I told him that if he stuck around long enough, maybe I would meet my future husband right there at my dad's center! By that Sunday morning, after two nights spent in constant vigilance that his time was running out, I was exhausted. My brother and his wife arrived and when he saw how haggard and exhausted I was, he said, "You know, I heard somewhere that people want to die on their own." I took that comment to mean that I was hindering or impeding Dad's passing because I did not want to leave him at night.

I left soon after that to go back to my parents' home. During breakfast, I found myself thinking, *Am I doing the right thing?* I was so beside myself that I questioned my faith and everything that I had strongly believed in up until that point in time. Was it all in my mind?

I took the day to regroup. I packed my bag and went back to the hospice center at 5:00 pm that night. My brother informed me that Dad had never woken up during the day while he was there. When I arrived, the aide told me he had woken up, summoned her, and she put him in a chair. She said he ate a snack of fruit and cake leftover from my brother's shift. That was hard to believe because as I walked in the room, he was sleeping, looking like a frail bird. He woke up and asked me where he was. Somewhere in there his words included, "Same game plan, you bring the meals?" I said yes.

I asked if he was hungry. He said no and drifted back to sleep. I gently removed his hearing aids and dentures. An odd whim prompted me to change the TV channel and watch a movie by his side, just for a few moments. For a short while, I escaped into that film, losing track of time and where I was. I wasn't in a hospice center, my father wasn't dying, and I did not feel like a girl without a home. It was just a peaceful Sunday night. He woke up with a start and asked, "What are we doing?" I immediately asked if he needed anything and told him I was watching the end of a movie.

He replied, "Are you serious? I'm paying two hundred dollars a night for this shit." That was his roundabout terse way of telling me he was ready for me to allow him to transition. I immediately turned off the TV and kissed him on the head. He drifted off to sleep. I was crying. I thought, *Am I crazy? Is this really happening?*

I saw a volunteer who was a professor by day at one of the local universities outside my dad's room. I asked him the burning question, "Do people want to die alone?" Would you want to die alone?" I had to know... was my dad waiting for me to leave, or did he want me to stay? This loving man looked at me and said, "Oh, no, for me, I would want someone with me at the end." I had my answer. I went into what I called the great room by the fireplace and wrote him my final goodbye letter.

I told him I had everything in place. Everything that I felt he would worry about I had taken care of. My only request was to spend one more night with him, and if I could, to accompany him as far as possible before letting him go. He granted my wish. At 4:30 am Monday, July 2nd, I heard him pass right next to me as the darkness was lifting into light. That wise professor, even though he was a complete stranger... I knew God sent him at the perfect time to assure me I was on the right path. If it wasn't for him, I might not have stayed the night. I have never experienced so much love and peace as I did in that room. The aide came in soon after Dad had moved on to check on us. She confirmed what I already knew. He was gone.

My greatest gift and manifestation yet had played out beautifully. So, I'm here to tell you, if there is anything you have doubts about, just ask... the Universe will provide you with the answer you're on the right path. All you have to do is keep an open mind and heart and look!

diana.previs1@gmail.com

PINKK on POINT: Letting go is the path to sustainable kindness in the universe.

GRATEFUL
BY DALE FRIEDMAN

I am grateful for the support I received during my journey of professional and personal development. Professionally, the turning point in my career occurred when I was promoted to a position for which I felt unqualified. My boss explained that my good managerial skills brought about the promotion, adding that a good manager does not have to be an expert in the fields one manages.

I had always heard that a good salesperson can sell anything. I was in technology, and prior to that time did not realize that what applies to sales also applies to management. Consequently, my goals (and achievements) expanded, and I never again felt unqualified for a promotion. This all led to my professional (and monetary) advancement, and I am forever grateful.

Personally, I am grateful to my childhood friend who taught (and continues to teach) me invaluable lessons in friendship, faith, and love. My friend and I were born within days of one another. Our mothers were high school friends, became new wives and mothers together, and friendship seemed our destiny. In grammar school, we were best friends.

In junior high, my friend's mother died of cancer. I supported her (she supported me, too) in ways that 13-year-olds support one another when experiencing loss previously inconceivable. Within a year, her family moved away. We no longer went to the same school or knew each other's friends, but we stayed in contact. After high school, I went to college, and she went to work in California. After college, I moved to Chicago, as did she, and we reestablished our friendship.

However, we were on very different personal journeys. She got married, moved to the suburbs, and raised a family while I continued my climb up the corporate ladder. We only had our history in common.

Yet every year she would call to wish me a happy birthday (years after I no longer responded or reciprocated). I had many childhood friends with whom I was no longer in contact with, as she did. I had not seen or spoken with this friend in over 15 years.

Almost 10 years ago, I saw my friend's sister who informed me my friend had received a breast cancer diagnosis and underwent a full mastectomy. Shortly before that, I received my birthday phone call as usual. She said in her message she was sick (her voice sounded weak) and so could not sing me *Happy Birthday* (as she did every year). She added that she hoped the next time I saw her would not be on her deathbed.

Her sister told me she made that call while in the hospital. I still didn't call her back, fearful that our next contact would be from her deathbed. I promised myself and promised God when she recovered, I would see her because I truly wanted to, not because she was ill.

Over six months passed before I learned that she had fully recovered. I also found out she'd be performing at an upcoming event (her sister told me she had been singing with a band prior to her illness). I attended it and surprised her. I asked her why she continued to reach out to me when I never replied. She told me I was worth it. We are best friends once again. She remains cancer-free. I remain her biggest fan (personally and professionally). We've supported one another through my mother and her sister's deaths, both due to cancer. Together we've celebrated her daughter's college graduation, our 50th birthdays, and every birthday, year after year.

Every day I try to prove to her, to all my friends and family, to God, and to myself, that I *am* worth it. I have become a better friend and a better person. I am truly grateful.

dfriedman65@gmail.com

PINKK on POINT: Kindness has no requirements or expectations. It is just kind-and creates friendships in unexpected ways.

GALVANIZED
BY CECIL ANNE BOOTH

My word is "galvanized", which means to inspire and/or ignite. There was not one pivotal moment in my journey. No one "aha moment" like the ones Oprah likes to share. Instead, my journey has been a series of steps and missteps layered, then stripped away and then layered some more. This eventually galvanized me to become the woman I knew I could be.

One thing that has always held true for me is a yearning to go places; to do more, and perhaps most of all, to seek fulfillment. From a young age, I had a desire to see the world, not just to travel but to learn and experience. I spent a good part of my youth in the middle; not high, not low.

I lived in the middle of the country in a middle-class family smack dab in the middle of five children. There weren't too many opportunities as I was growing up to get out of the middle other than through books and dreams. Transitioning through the neighborhood public high school to college at the affordable state school the middle persisted, but so did the yearning.

Breaking out of the Middle

The first breakout moment for me came when I was about to graduate college. I realized to get out of the middle I would have to get my ticket stamped some place outside of my home state. I applied to graduate schools, tapping into my budding interest in journalism and communications. Soon after I packed my tiny car with a few belongings and moved to Chicago, a place I'd never been. Not quite out of the middle, but certainly more diverse and exciting.

With my passport in life stamped a year later, I landed a job that opened the door to experiencing and funding my "searcher" mentality. I also got an actual passport and within a year, was off to France, the first destination on my list of places and cultures to experience. It did not disappoint. I found that I could go anywhere from my home base in Chicago, experience other parts of the U.S. and the world, and then come back to a great job, home, and eventually a family.

Answering the Call of Mother Nature

Somewhere in my thirties I realized, *I better get going if I want to have a child*. Since one of my sisters is an OB/GYN I had the inside scoop on managing fertility. I realized then that while women are living much longer, we can now be more strategic about motherhood and career. The biological clock is real and ticking, and we must keep that in mind while we pursue all of our goals. But we have more options now. Stay tuned, as my sister also later inspired me in many other ways.

Back to the call for motherhood. The guy I was dating when I had this realization seemed reasonably well suited—good looking, smart and fun. There was no lightning bolt, but time was ticking. Marriage followed, and within a few years, so did a beautiful baby girl. I was still working full time, still yearning for life experiences, and now, I was even better equipped to "do it all."

But then there came a minor hiccup. The ideal man didn't turn out to be the right life partner. So, I had to make one of the toughest decisions of my life—to end that marriage. I won't call this a misstep as it gave me the gift of my daughter, a person I consider one of my two biggest accomplishments in life. It was, however, one of those life-changing moments that makes you reassess.

I had an amicable divorce, am still friendly with my ex-husband and boringly, and have no story of woe to tell about that chapter of my life. To be clear, however, this was a choice I made. It could have become dark and ugly. I had seen this happen to friends and to my own mother. I knew that a negative path would not serve my daughter or me. Therefore, I made the choice to not let that wrinkle in my and my daughter's life stories cause us to miss a beat.

Second Acts

Happily going about my life plan with my daughter in tow, my fabulous job continued as did the great travel and experiences. I wanted for nothing more. Then along came an English chap visiting friends in Chicago. His arrival and our connection produced that lightning bolt I had yet to experience when I least expected it. I certainly wasn't seeking it, but it struck, undeniably. I found myself both conflicted and excited. But did I really want to go down the marriage path again? Would it be good for me and my four-year-old daughter? Then again, could we afford not to take such chances?

The Englishman moved to Chicago and within a year we were engaged. Within two years we had a baby son, my second biggest accomplishment. To clarify, I don't feel that having children was the accomplishment. Rather it was raising them, learning from them, and passing along my many life experiences, both great and terrible—those serve as the accomplishment. Most of all, I wanted to show them they could work and seek their own dreams and also raise children and that this would not be a sacrifice.

A second act came along with my career as well. Sometimes life moments lead you in new directions. Finding a best friend and soulmate in my forties was an eye-opener. What else was possible? Having a second baby at 40 was not in the life plan. It caused me to want to share this realization. That became possible in a conversation with my sister (remember the OB/GYN?) We had the shared experience of having children a little later in life than women are designed to do. She so beautifully shared with me that hormonal variation throughout our lifetimes hugely impacts us. Why do we not talk about that? It is not a deficit–it is a reality. We need to explore it, understand it and find ways to optimize. And if we can do that, share it with every woman we can!

Sharing the Wisdom is Not Enough

With this life experience and our shared professional experience, my sister and I created a mission statement to: Share the wisdom of the female cycle and provide solutions about how to live better in that knowledge. The first "product" is a book I urged my sister to write, *The Venus Week... Discover the Powerful Secret of your Cycle... at any Age (Da Capo 2008)*. In this book, she generously shares her experience as a doctor of women, seeing them throughout their lifetime and helping them with their most intimate challenges.

We learned from the editorial community that it is not enough to share wisdom, but we need practical and specific solutions. One friend that I soft sounded about this endeavor said to me, "That is all great to know, but what am I supposed to do with that information?" This pushback was extremely helpful, and I realized that one book is not enough. The writing and editing uncovered many unmet needs for women we needed to talk about and help to solve. I left that amazing job of twenty years and started a company with my sister to share the wisdom and the solutions.

The Venus Effect

What grew from these discoveries, guided by friends, sisters and mentors, is a platform in women's beauty and wellness. *The Venus Week* helped take the focus off the negative aspects of our cycle and shine the light on the time when we are at our peak. Mother Nature gave us a gift of fertility and to help pave the way, the week leading up to ovulation holds the secrets of optimal hormonal vitality. During this magical week, from our young teens until around age 50, we have a lift in estrogen that helps with skin, verbal acuity, carbohydrate metabolism, sleep, and energy. We are simply meant to look and feel great when we are about to ovulate. But we don't want that just for that one fleeting week—and certainly we want to feel vital well after age 50! That is what we call the Venus Effect and why we named our skin care range VENeffect.

We focused on skincare because it was the white space in beauty that no one was addressing. Why are hormones negatively perceived and cast? It has been going on for centuries. Menopause is the *absence* of estrogen, or what my sister calls the "ovarian retirement plan". We should not vilify estrogen but instead look for ways to mimic its beauty safely. We chose to tap into the plant world and developed our line with natural plant-based phytoestrogens. Molecules that come from the reproductive part of the plan and, on skin, can signal the machinery of supple luminous skin. Medical research has studied this for years. We simply found cosmetically available forms and created skin care products that are potent yet gentle and safe, to give us that Venus glow.

We have been selling our line of skin care in the beauty world for several years now, and in several countries. We are competing with the giants, but one thing holds true: all women on the planet are affected by hormonal varia-tion and there are few solutions to this universal need. We are working extremely hard and are still building awareness, with our original mission in mind – serving women.

Next Generation

Our daughters were six and eight when we began to plan our business and they are now in their twenties, both working in New York. There were many years where we questioned, is all this hard work really worth it? Are we compromising our roles as mothers and wives to follow this path? And our kids sometimes questioned our time as well. What we know now is that we really were teach-ing them about following a path – no matter how hard – with the goal, not of monetary gain (although there were jokes about the VENeffect yacht that has not yet surfaced), of satisfaction that you were looking to do something good in the world.

We, in effect, we're doing this to pay it forward to the next generation. Not just so that they would have access to more enlightened ways to navigate hormonal change, but to show that work and perseverance are rewarding, and we should not settle for what others impose, but seek to find the beauty of finding authenticity.

That desire to seek fulfillment never goes away. For me, it is a constant looking forward at what is next. Well into my fifties now, I feel I have so much more to learn, experience and share. For the cup is half full.

cecilbooth@veneffect.com

PINKK on POINT: Sharing wisdom and knowledge permeates kindness and beauty. Beauty is kindness.

PURPOSEFUL
BY TITA ARROYO

I've always felt that I have a big purpose—to help others; to be a "light" to others.

My parents led by example by being kind and always providing encouragement and guidance to everyone they knew. A simple smile, saying "good morning" or asking a question can make someone's day—on purpose. Everyone is important and we should help everyone feel their importance.

In my twenties, I joined a direct sales company that provides a positive, encouraging and empowering platform for women. Being part of that environment and having a strong faith-filled, believing mentor reignited my passion for that bigger purpose I felt. Along my journey, I've made it a point to continue being that encourager and enthusiastic believer of everyone's paths and dreams. However, there was still a lingering question: *How can I truly make an impact?*

Unimaginably, I received a little more clarity about my purpose when illness fell upon family members. This began with my dad, who suffered a fatal, massive heart attack at age fifty-four. In shock, my purpose shifted to cultivating a healthier lifestyle. I started doing a lot of research regarding illness, food supply, ingredients, and sharing with anyone interested. One major discovery for me was that if there is less than one percent of any ingredient in a product, the product label does not have to disclose that. *Wait, What?*

How can we know what is truly in a product? They add chemicals and colorants to improve shelf life and make products more visually appealing. That does not mean that the products are safe. Product labels are confusing, stating "natural", "sugar-free", "fat-free", and "healthy" although the ingredient list will prove otherwise (if it's even complete). There is no regulation to use these words to describe and market products. The U.S. allows the use of ingredients banned in other countries in our products. How can we know that something we are ingesting or putting on our skin is not causing an allergy or contributing to an illness?

Round two of my purpose shaping was coming. A few years later, my mom got a rare blood cancer, and in what seemed like minutes, she was gone. A month later, one of my sisters (age 41) was diagnosed with stage one breast cancer (she's thankfully in remission). My mom and sister both had fairly healthy eating habits, worked out regularly, and had no other illness. How did they both get cancer? Having lost my father 11 years prior, all of this really shook me. I'm only in my mid-thirties—how can both of my parents be gone? All the prior research kept me asking myself: Is there a link between ingredients in our food and personal/household products and illness? This is when my shift arrived, and I could not ignore it. What was I going to do to help myself and others lead a healthier, happier, more balanced, LONGER life?

I decided it was time to take control of what goes *on* my body, not just what goes in. I began making my own natural soaps and lip balms and started my own natural products company, Life Loves Co. My mission is to help others start or stay on their journey to a happy, healthy, and balanced life—Naturally! I want to help everyone achieve a healthier and more natural lifestyle. Although purposeful, how do I make that bigger impact I've always searched for?

A lot of reflecting and research revealed my bigger purpose! I am thrilled to be in a program to become a Functional Medicine Certified Health Coach, enabling me to coach others to make the positive changes they want and need to lead their healthiest and happiest lives. I'll be purposefully leading myself and others to the life of light that is everyone's birthright. I'm so excited to impact lives positively with my "light" and passion for helping others.

Don't give up on your purpose. Remember to ask and wait. I promise the answers will always come! Be the light in someone else's day, especially when it's hardest, on those days that you need that for yourself. Follow through on purposefully lighting up someone's day, and you'll see it lights up others and yourself along the journey. My light shines bright and my purpose is stronger than ever. Did you catch a spark?! I'd love to hear about it! Leave me a note at www.lifelovesco.com. Cheers to your best life!

Don't give up on your purpose. My light shines brightly, and my purpose is stronger than ever.

Life Loves Co-Founder

info@lifelovesco.com

PINKK on POINT: A purposeful life begets kindness.

INTUITION
BY CHERYL E. BOOTH

While deciding which story of kindness to share from a plethora of personal examples, I followed my intuition. I chose one about a remarkable person from my early life, my Aunt Kathleen. She had an amazing sense of humor and a huge, boisterous laugh (similar to comedienne Phyllis Diller's) which I could hear echoing in my head when I telepathically told her one reason I chose her as the subject my contribution to this book. Kathleen was married five times, but the surname she had the longest was Kaiser. So, her initials were KK, and when I realized those are right in the PINKK acronym, it just felt like confirmation.

This incident of kindness dates back to 1960, so I'll give a bit more recent retrospective before we time travel all the way back 60 years.

Backstory Perspective: In 1982, I moved from Missouri to California, intending to make it big in the music and acting industry. In the Midwest, I had sung in bands professionally for more than a decade and played the lead role in several musicals. While I was on a set break at many gigs, or when the band was breaking down instruments, several people would come up to me saying, "Man! You are so talented! Why don't you go to New York or

L.A.? Someplace you'd have a better shot of catching a break."

I'd already been considering that for quite a while. There are only so many hotel lounges and dive bars where you can perform before you resign yourself to, "This is as good as it's ever going to get." I refused to accept that. My older sister lived in the L.A. area and had invited me to come live with her, so I took a leap of faith and headed west.

Childhood: My Aunt Kathy was always supportive of my singing. Her two sons were already adults, so when her older sister Dolores (Dee) had a baby girl, Aunt Kathy became a force of nature in my young life. We lived in Gladstone, Missouri, a suburb of Kansas City. Kathy and Uncle John lived on their farm in Goodland, Kansas. To my dismay, we couldn't make the six-hour drive often, but thankfully she came to visit us fairly frequently.

She always asked me to sing songs and reenact some of my favorite movie or TV scenes, and she would applaud and cheer. Always a big ham, I took several bows and curtain calls whenever she was around. My Pentecostal parents usually reserved their praise for those times I would choose a gospel number or a hymn. That was fine, but not a genre that made my heart soar, even as a little kid.

I nicknamed her "Aunt Khaki" when I was around two years old. She loved it and insisted that I call her that until I grew too "embarrassed and sophisticated," somewhere around age 8. Knowing I was a bookworm who loved music, she always brought me a book or record when she visited. Since I was a true tomboy, sometimes she took me shopping for jeans and tennis shoes. This earned her a disapproving look from Mom, who had hoped her only daughter would be a prim and proper little Miss. Gosh darn, sorry 'bout that, Mom! (*Not really*)

Kathy gave me many books over the years. *The Wizard of Oz* was my favorite movie of all time (still is, actually) and so Aunt Kathy gave me the entire series of L. Frank Baum's Oz books. She took the time to get to know me, which is so important for adults to do with kids. Those books remain one of my most cherished collectibles. She favored me with many acts of kindness, not just material gifts. When she sat down to converse with me, she made great eye contact and talked to me like I was an adult. Never dismissive or condescending.

To this day, I remember that kindness and am grateful. And oh yes, she was definitely the most colorful relative I had. She loved to go to Las Vegas to gamble and see shows (shocking my mother!) and I remember vividly that she swore like a sailor and smoked like a chimney! Such an amazing character. She will always hold a special place in my heart.

The most touching act of kindness she extended towards our family, however, was unexpected, unique, and deeply appreciated. It took place in a hospital waiting room.

Shortly after I turned four years old, my mom excitedly told me she was going to have a baby. I found out much later that this pregnancy was unplanned, since she was nearly 43 and my father was 58. Still and all, she was happy about it, and so was I. I started chirping about how great it would be when my baby brother got here. Mind you, this was 1960, long before prenatal gender identification technology even existed.

Sidebar: Since the age of two, I've had vivid precognitive dreams. I'd regale my poor mother about them over the breakfast table, sharing things like, "We're moving to a pink house, Mama. I saw it in a dream." She laughed it off, saying, "Oh, Cheryl, all little girls want to live in a pink house." I shook my head no. "Huh-uh. You know my favorite color is blue. But I saw this house, and it's pink. Oh! And it has a chimbley on the roof. I saw smoke coming out of it!" She laughed again and dismissed it. That is until the one house that my father could afford in his search for a bigger home turned out to be pink; and yes, it had a fireplace.

If you think that didn't cause Dolores to give me a side-long glance of curiosity tinged and peevishness, think again. (FYI, one of the first things she demanded when we moved was that my father paint the new house yellow, as if to obliterate my psychic accuracy).

Back to Mom & Me: A new baby! I was beside myself with glee. I envisioned us playing all kinds of sports and games, putting on little plays—this was going to be great! I excitedly told her, "I can't wait for my brother to get here, Mama. Oh, and he's saying his name is Johnny. Can we please name him Johnny, please?" She laughed a bit, in too good of a mood to scold me for what she took for childish foolishness. "Oh, my goodness, Cheryl Ellen. What makes you think it's a boy? There's no way to know that. And your best friend's name is Johnny, so that's where you're getting that. How on earth can you possibly imagine a baby in Mommy's tummy is talking to you? I swear, child." She chuckled, but I shook my head no.

"I'm telling you, Mama, he *is* talking to me." Her good mood started to fade as the smile fled from her face. Uh-oh. From experience, I knew better than to push it much further. "Um, if the baby is a boy, could we please call him Johnny, though? I think he'd like that." She sighed. "Well, let's ask your daddy when he gets home from work. I'm sure he'll be okay with it. When has he ever refused to go along with your ideas?"

The designated family disciplinarian, Mom subscribed to the "spare the rod, spoil the child" theory. By age four I'd been spanked not only by her firm, strong hand, but with a hairbrush, a razor strop–*that REALLY hurt*–and pretty much whatever was within reach when she felt I needed a few swats. I was usually punished for things I said, not actions; typically when I was talking about things she didn't fully understand or if she thought I was just mouthing off at her.

As she was spanking me, she often rhythmically grunted with each swat, "Straighten. Up. And. Fly. Right." I'd hold my breath so as not to cry, and that only made her swing with more velocity. I didn't know how to fly right, or that it was the name of a song until years later. I don't blame her now and have forgiven that behavior. It's how my grandmother raised her.

Back then, I just knew my daddy never laid a finger on me, even if he was mad for a few seconds. He was my champion, told great jokes, and was one of my best friends. For the rest of his life, we had a special bond; not to mention, I pretty much look like my dad in drag! I'm serious. Friends that have seen pictures of him and then looked back at me have said as much. But I don't mind. He was a good-looking fellow! That was another thing that irritated Mom—her only girl didn't resemble her "one iota."

When Dad got home from work, she ran the name suggestion by him. "Sit down, Walt, and hold on to your hat. You won't believe this. Cheryl's convinced the baby is a boy and insists he's telling her he wants his name to be Johnny." "His name IS Johnny," I mumbled. She shot a glare at me, but Dad smiled. "Well, I think Johnny is a good name. But tell you what, Punkin, could we give him my middle name of Howard? Do you think he'll like that?" His blue eyes twinkled as he glanced at his wife and then back to his daughter. I clapped my hands. "Oh, yes, Daddy! I know he'll like being named after you!" I ran to give him a hug. He always gave great ones.

Fast Forward—July 8, 1960. Dad rushed us to the hospital as soon as Mom's water broke. I remember sitting in the waiting room with him, swinging my legs while working on some *Highlights* magazine puzzles. I kept rubbing my nose because the antiseptic smell was so strong. Daddy was pacing back and forth, as fathers do in that circumstance. At one point, the doctor came out and pulled Dad aside, talking in hushed tones.

When the doctor left, my father slowly walked back in my direction. His looked like a lost little boy. I jumped up and took his hand. "Daddy, are Mama and Johnny okay? What's the matter?" He cleared his throat and composed himself, scooping me up in his arms and managing a smile. "They're fine, Cheryl. And yes, Johnny's a boy. You were right." He gave me a quick kiss on the forehead, but I could tell he was distracted, and that this wasn't the time to ask him a ton of questions.

We saw Mama a couple of hours later. She looked small and weak in that hospital bed; I'd never seen her like that. I crossed to her side and held her hand, quiet as a mouse. She said, "You be a good girl for your daddy, honey. The baby and me have to stay here for a few days, but you'll come visit. It'll be all right. We'll be home before you know it. I need you to be my brave girl. Can you do that?" I nodded and then asked, "But Mama, where is Johnny? Why isn't he here in the room with you?" A tear rolled down her cheek and my dad quickly stepped in. "Oh, he needs some special attention, kiddo, so he's with the nurses and doctors. They're taking good care of him, don't you worry."

"But why can't they come home now?" "Soon, baby, soon," my mom said, her eyelids drooping. "I have to get some sleep, and so does Johnny. You'll come back in the morning and things will be better." "That's right, Cheryl. You stop that silly worrying right now!" Dad assured me as he swung me up onto his shoulder, making me laugh.

We went home for supper and a few hours' sleep. The next few days we spent most of our time at the hospital. Eating at the cafeteria was fun until I reached my Jell-O tolerance limit. Sometimes there were other kids in the waiting room that I could talk to and play games with. Dad talked to several doctors, always just out of earshot. They looked so serious and shook my father's hand after talking, as though to give him extra support. We visited Mama for a little while every day, and I believe it was about the third day into this new routine that they finally allowed me to see my brother. He was beautiful!

Johnny had a shock of jet-black hair, same as I had in my baby pictures. He was so tiny, and Mama held onto him like she'd never let him go whenever the nurses handed him to her. But they didn't let her keep him for long. My parents explained that he had to receive lots of medicine and stay in an incubator sometimes to keep him warm. I knew this was odd and part of me wanted to scream, "What's wrong with my baby brother? Why can't we take him home NOW?!?" But I knew better and was on my best behavior.

One day as we were in the lobby, giving Mama time to rest, a familiar voice rang out cheerfully, "Is that my big girl Cheryl I see?" I brightened up immediately. "Aunt Khaki!" I squealed, running to hug her tightly. I somehow knew she and my dad were exchanging meaningful serious looks over my head. He walked up and hugged her, saying, "Thank you for coming, Kathleen. It means the world to us."

She reached in her purse and pulled out a bag of red licorice, one of my favorites. "Here you go, Tiger," she said, handing it to me. "I have to talk with your daddy now. This should keep you busy." She grinned, and I sat down, biting into a piece of the chewy treat. They chatted—again, out of earshot. After a few minutes, Kathleen stood up. "Okay, I'm going to see my big sis and this gorgeous baby boy." I ran to her side. "I want to go with you!" She looked down at me, cupping my chin in her hand and making direct eye contact. "We'll all have time to spend together, when the doctors say it's all right for them to come home. But right now, they say it's best for Dee if she just has one visitor at a time. Okay, honey?" I nodded. "Sure. I just can't wait 'til we're all back home."

"That's how we all feel," she agreed. "And hey, guess what? I'll stay at your house for a week or two to help out." "Oh, goody!" I cheered. Kathleen gave my shoulder a squeeze and headed off to visit her sister. Dad and I resumed our stations in the lobby. After about a half-hour, my aunt emerged, wiping her eyes quickly with a tissue. She wadded it up and stuffed it in her purse, hoping I hadn't seen. I jumped up and started running toward her, and then froze, watching this all unfold. It confirmed my suspicions that something was off kilter. Aunt Khaki was like my mom; tough as nails most of the time. I'd never seen her cry about anything. Still, I had received orders from Sergeant Mom to "be a good girl," and that usually meant zip your lip, so I fought the impulse to ask a lot of questions. Kathy empathically felt my worries. She took my hand, leading me back to my chair.

Sitting beside me, she nodded to the chair on my other side, indicating that Dad should sit there. He did, and she took a deep breath. "Well, honey, I know you're wondering what in the world is going on. If it's okay with your daddy, I'll do my best to explain it. Is that all right, Walt?" He nodded. He hadn't felt up to giving me any report about what was going on, and I knew that. His eyes had teared up several times, and that scared me. My daddy never cried, either. I looked at my aunt, who was smoothing her skirt, searching for the right thing to say to her precocious little niece.

"Okay, so here goes. The doctors are calling Johnny's condition a 'birth injury.' That means he needs lots of special care." She paused, and Dad nodded slightly, giving her permission to go ahead. "He has something called cerebral palsy, Cheryl. He's having lots of these nasty things called seizures, and they're trying to get those under control before they let him and your mama come home." She paused, looking around. "Oh, good! *There's* the drinking fountain. Stay put. Be right back." She walked deliberately toward the fountain, took a long drink and slowly returned to sit beside me. I'm sure she was stalling for time; formulating how to explain all of this to a 4-year-old without upsetting me.

"But Aunt Khaki, what's a seizure?" I blurted out. She smiled kindly, knowing I was full of curiosity and concern. "Well, they explained it like this—sometimes the wiring in Johnny's brain gets mixed up somehow, and he shakes pretty hard and can't stop for a while." I heard my dad's throat catch and stifle a sob, and he got up to get a drink of water, too. While he stepped away, my aunt told me that the baby would need lots of love and attention, and some medicine to make those stupid seizure things stop. Those weren't her exact words, but it's how I translated them.

"Oh, I'll do anything I can to make him better. I've waited for him for so long." She hugged me tight. "I know that, Sugar. You will be the best big sister anybody has ever seen. Johnny is very lucky to have you." I nodded, confident I could live up to her faith in me, no matter what.

She fished around in her purse, pulling out a fat sealed envelope. "Now, I'll see you all back at the house. I'll get supper started, so we can all have a good meal. Enough of this hospital crap, right?" I laughed. Now *that* sounded like Aunt Khaki! She stood up, gave me another quick hug, and handed the envelope to Dad. He tried to refuse it, but she wasn't having any of that. "Look here, Walt," she said firmly. "You all will have a ton of doctor bills. I wish I could contribute a thousand times more, but for now, this will have to do. Use it however you need, and I don't want to hear any more about it. We all need a little help sometimes, and Brother Walter, you guys really need it now. I'm happy I can do at least this much. Oh, and that's a gift, not a loan, you got it?" Dad silently took the envelope and gave her a hug. "Okay, thank you. We'll see you back at the house," he said quietly.

She turned on her heel and briskly headed towards the big red Exit sign, giving a backward wave over her shoulder as she left. Dad and I sat down, and he slowly opened the envelope. Tears welled up in his eyes once again as he counted it. "$500," he whispered. "Oh, my God. Your Aunt Kathleen is something else, I tell you." (In 1960, $500 had the purchasing power of somewhere over $4,000 in today's world). Aunt Kathleen was the only relative that ever helped with Johnny's expenses, at least that I know of. Grandma Bertha, Kathleen and Dolores' mother, was pretty well-to-do from having "married well" a few times. I know for a fact she could have come up with a lot more funds far easier than Kathy and Uncle John did. But that's another story.

Although Johnny never walked and spoke only a handful of words as the years went by, we immediately became best friends. One of my favorite shared activities was reading him some great books by Mark Twain, Louisa May Alcott, Laura Ingalls Wilder, and of course, all of those wonderful Oz books. I always did my best to do all the character voices to keep him entertained. When I was 10, my older brother gave me a piano for my birthday, and then playing and singing to Johnny was another fun bonding thing. Mom would often encourage me to go play outside, but more often than not, I stayed on the couch with Johnny. We loved and accepted each other unconditionally, and nothing felt better than that.

He was an amazing soul, and I am so blessed that he was my little brother for 25 years. I told him many times I would write a book about him someday, because I knew there was so much more to him than people saw on the surface. He wasn't to be pitied. He was one of the happiest, sweetest persons I've ever known and loved. He had a lot to give the world. I did write that book in 2006. It's called *Johnny Angel is My Brother, A Psychic Medium's Journey.* It's still on Amazon, and I plan to release an updated version in 2020.

Now: I gave singing and acting my best shot in L.A. during the 1980s. But my calling was that of a psychic medium. I do readings for people grieving over losing a loved one, or who need clarity from angels and spirit guides regarding life issues. I'm also a hypnotherapist, life coach, and I offer a psychic mentoring program. That was my primary vocation for 35 years; now I do it part-time. I'm happy to be of service that way, but my primary passion now is writing. I've been published in four books under my own name so far and ghostwritten more than I can count. I love writing screenplays, and one of my goals for the next two years is to get at least one screenplay sold and produced by 2021. Stay tuned and please hold that vision with me. Thank you.

Aunt Kathleen shall absolutely always be one of my favorite people. Stubborn, strong-willed, funny, even bawdy. Loving, kind, and constant in her acceptance of me and our mutual admiration society. Even though she wasn't a churchgoer like my mom, she had a heart of gold and understood the meaning of compassion and kindness better than most people who show up and sit in a pew every Sunday. "I love you to pieces, Aunt Khaki!" I sometimes shout to the heavens. I send the same message to my parents and my beloved Johnny nearly every day. They're all in heaven, and the amazing ways they have supported me from that dimension are—well, miraculous.

Thanks for reading this book. PINKK is a wonderful organization, and I am honored Melissa and Athena asked me to be a contributor here. All the women who have shared their powerful stories are incredible souls, and so are you!

God bless you. Remember, trust your own intuition every chance you get. It will never steer you wrong. It's a gift, and nothing to be afraid of. It's a rewarding life-altering journey, and even if you don't know it, you're on the right path, exactly where you are in this moment. Trust. Love. And always spread Kindness. It costs nothing, but its value is immeasurable.

www.cherylbooth.wordpress.com

www.shiningwrite.wordpress.com

Lifeofspirit@gmail.com

PINKK on POINT: Miracles are created by kindness. Trust that intuition of kindness.

BELIEF
BY KATHY MCCABE

When I was in my early 30s, I worked at a law firm. I had been working 70-hour weeks, and getting good results on cases, yet I didn't get the votes needed to make partner. Crushed that I didn't reach that goal, I wanted to know why and scheduled a meeting with my mentor. He said to me, "We can't get there alone." Wow. This mentor insightfully told me that my colleagues didn't know me and that I had shut people out. As I painfully listened to his feedback, I knew he was right. I changed how I showed up at work, became more collaborative, and made partner the following year.

Even though I was now a partner, I was miserable. I didn't like my work. I longed to have kids. I was dating a great guy who wanted to get married. The problem was marriage didn't feel right. I was in therapy but felt stuck and unhappy, like I wasn't going anywhere.

Seeing an ad in the church bulletin about creating a magical life, I broke out of my comfort zone and signed up for a course called "The Artist's Way." *The Artist's Way* is a self-help book by American author Julia Cameron. Cameron wrote the book to help people with artistic creative recovery—which essentially means helping people gain self-confidence through harnessing their creative talents and skills. That, in turn helps develop more confidence, insight, and wisdom. And it opens one's eyes to possibilities and what could be—if we let it. Our teacher was Paulette, a 50-something dynamic, joyful woman who had been down that dark, depressing road of pleasing everyone but herself. She had successfully learned to break those rules.

Paulette had gotten married at 16, divorced in her 40s, and was a single mom who worked as a nurse. However, she left nursing because it wasn't her passion. She completely changed her life and began doing work that changed and inspired people. She lived her life with complete joy and possibility. According to her, she wasn't wealthy and didn't have "connections," yet she made her dreams happen. She created a living that changed and inspired people; she took that two-week solo trip to Paris she wanted to take, went bungee jumping with her 14-year-old grandson, dated men who wanted to marry her, and stopped volunteering at church because she had thought she "had to."

Paulette was my inspiration, and she and the course were where I started to think differently about myself, my goals, my life, and my beliefs.

Our beliefs can move us forward or keep us stuck. Just like Paulette's head had been, my head was full of shoulds and "supposed tos"—i.e. I am "supposed to do, act or be" a certain way.

The problem was my "supposed tos" didn't align with my true self. What I really yearned for was freedom, connection and purpose. I had so many beliefs, especially unconscious ones, that were keeping me stuck and unhappy.

While I didn't immediately quit my job, I did start working differently. I focused more on what I liked to do and did less of what I didn't like. I got promoted and worked less. I married the guy that felt right. In my early 40s, I became a mom of two through adoption. I finally quit my legal job and stayed at home to be with my kids.

For fun, I led my own "Artist's Way" course and saw the magic of 10 women who started making inspirational changes in their lives. This group inspired me to become a life coach.

Today *I* am that 50-something women who works with others to create magical lives. I continue to be a work-in-progress creation, but I am attuned to following what feels right for me, not what society says I should be or do.

Kathy@kathymccabelifecoach.com

PINKK on POINT: Kindness is magic. Magic is kindness. Just believe.

BRAVE
BY JEN SCHERBAUER

ravery. It's something with which we are born into this world; from our first breath to our first step; to taking off the training wheels to our first day of school. As children, we embrace bravery and adults encourage us to be brave. Bravery drives experience, learning, and growth. Later on in life, little events such as asking that special person to prom, taking your driver's test, and finally going off to college are all too often undermined as not being "brave," but they are. They are an active choice to take risks instead of remaining in your comfort zone. Throughout life, we as women take tons of risks every day that go unacknowledged, because as we grow older, the connotation of "brave" changes.

When you think of the word "brave," what comes to mind? In an online poll, 60% of people named a *male* superhero, or a male influencer—a Native American male warrior or a male military officer. The connotation of the word brave, therefore, shifts to be that of courageous masculinity. I've seen this social shift in bravery move away from femininity throughout my life. As women, they teach us to be soft, gentle, and sweet… "sugar and spice and everything nice." And as women we are. But we are also brave.

Do you know what I think is brave? Vulnerability. I think honesty is brave. I think authenticity is brave. I think morality is brave. I think kindness is brave. I also think intelligence and hard work are brave. Overall, I think being a woman in today's world is EXTREMELY brave. We have so many expectations put on us in addition to all the hats we wear. One woman can be a nurse to her children, psychologist to her friends, cheerleader to her partner, chef and maid for her family, caretaker to her pets or children, and maybe even a professional in her career.

My story does not start out as one that invokes bravery. I grew up in the boonies of northeastern Ohio, raised by two very loving, well-to-do parents. Growing up, my life was full of love, encouragement, and wonderful opportunities, all of which I willingly took advantage. In this environment, I grew up as a tomboy—wrestling with my brother and cousins, not knowing a single girl outside of school. I broke numerous bones climbing trees, and my father nicknamed me "Amazing Grace" because, well, I was not.

It wasn't until high school that I began feeling pressure to have a certain "aesthetic." I went to a private school where wealth, beauty, and promiscuity were currency. Not ironically, beauty and wealth went hand-in-hand with promiscuity. If you were rich or promiscuous, beauty did not hold as much weight. But if you were average at all three, you were, well, average. I was average, but I was smart. Throughout my life, I learned to identify as being smart, blending my risk-taking nature with my wit and intellect.

This blend of characteristics afforded me the ability to assess the risks I took, even when those decisions or acts were difficult to make. Intelligence was great, but it made academics, well, boring. I was constantly looking for an adrenaline rush. For example, in my senior year of high school, I auditioned for the lead in the school musical (*Footloose*), tried out for the powderpuff football team, and ran for prom queen. I landed all three. In college, I became a paramedic, because apparently simply partying wasn't exciting enough for my weekends.

During my junior year, I decided to complete the liberal arts portion of my education in Greece. I enrolled, obtained a passport, and raised my living expenses all on my own, over the course of one year. I then proudly notified my parents on graduation move-out day that I would, in fact, not be coming home to Cleveland. Instead, I'd fly across the world to live for the following year. My risk assessment calculation did not account for my parents' shock and anger over my audacious and dangerous decision. But I went and had the most amazing experience of my life.

Following graduation, I enrolled in the Peace Corps and was stationed in Belize at a local clinic. They cancelled my tour after one year, but that was also an amazing though risky process and decision.

Then I decided to attend medical school in Chicago in my now late-twenties—leaving my boyfriend of six years behind along with my family. To add insult to injury, this was anything but a traditional medical school, disappointing most of my friends and my partner. Rather than a traditional medical school, I set my sights on a Naturopathic, Chiropractic, and Traditional Chinese Medical school. I intended to get doctorates in all three. It was difficult and ultimately risky, because the debt-to-income ratio is unsure with multiple degrees.

After graduating cum laude, I walked into my first job at a clinic in the Willis Tower, where I decided to start my own business in what was traditionally a man's profession. The amount of men and women who looked at my blonde, 5'2" frame and scoffed at my ability to adjust them or have any ability to diagnose or treat them was daunting. But patient after patient, day after day, I proved them wrong and earned their respect. After only six months of practice, having finally gained momentum in patient care, my clinic owner informed me that he was going to sell the practice. This left me again looking for a new job… in a man's profession.

Simultaneously, my boyfriend of five years and I went through a difficult breakup. We had moved in together only six months prior. I had to make the difficult and heartbreaking decision to leave him. This meant trying to afford an apartment on my own in the third largest city in the nation, compounded by the facts that I was in my midthirties and only had five months of income. Not impossible, but let me tell you, not easy.

After two weeks of job-hunting and apartment-hunting, they informed me that the sale of the clinic did not go through. This meant that I had to re-interview for my old position with the same boss, as I had not found another suitable option. I spent exactly two weeks figuratively single, homeless, and jobless in, yes, the third largest city in America.

This was the first time in my life I felt unsure of my future. I had always been on the same trajectory: go to college, go to medical school, find a job, help people, get married, and start a family. I have never self-pitied since I pride myself as a "fixer," which is why being a physician was an almost too-perfect career choice for me. During this time, I was inundated with Instagram posts about "manifesting" and "gratitude journals," but as an evidence-based physician, I really had a hard time getting behind it. However, something about it all was calling to me. So, I gave it a whirl. This was the pivotal turning point in my life. I bravely threw myself into the unknown and asked the universe to bring me an opportunity for stability, which was what I ultimately craved. And stability it gave me, but not without testing me.

I will admit, I walked into my job at the Willis Tower with little to no effort ONE YEAR before I actually started working. The head of my class, I had three doctorates, was head intern, and had a decent reputation in the profession. There was comfort and security, and frankly I couldn't conceive of anything that I didn't know. When the clinic sold, I'd be hit with the demotion of owning my own business to working *under* a man. I had been tailoring my career focused in functional medicine and women's health with prospects of eventual partnership or ownership, and like I said, it had started to pick up steam. I would forfeit all of that, none of which I wanted or was ready to do.

But just as I was about to sign a contract out of desperation, I got a call. Some investors had heard about me and wanted to 'gift' me a clinic and to hire me on as a full-time clinic director. They showed full faith in me, despite my limited amount of time in practice. They believed I was ready to take on the responsibilities of owning my clinic.

If you are unaware of all that it takes to run a practice, I won't bore you. Just know, there's a LOT that goes into it. A lot that medical school doesn't teach upcoming physicians because we're too busy learning the human body and its intricacies. THIS was daunting, and I had only five days to decide where to put my signature—on one contract or the other. There was so much risk to up and leaving my current practice and take on running one, which I had only a smidge of the knowledge to do. It was heart-wrenching to treat my patients, knowing I would be leaving them, wondering if they would follow. But I took the leap. I took the risk. And it has paid off.

Granted, change always comes with a degree of loss. In my breakup, I lost not just my partner but my best friend of five years. With the decision to run my own clinic, I lost some patients and comfort in what I had created. But when you "lose" something, you make space for something new. The good news is, I've found that the universe generally makes sure it's better. And in this case, that's exactly what happened.

I am still learning to find love. As a 30-something professional, dating is far from easy. Opening up again, telling your story *over and over* can be exhausting. You will need to kiss frogs (yes, you *will* kiss many frogs) before finding a prince or two. But the process has its own beauty, and you must embrace your exposure to those experiences.

What these stories have taught me is that I am braver than I ever thought, and that bravery comes in *so* many forms. I've been so inspired to witness bravery in others. I often reflect on my source of bravery; where it came from, who inspired me. When it boils down to it, I have to thank my mother. Mind you, this is not a heartwarming, mutually loving relationship. I will wholeheartedly tell you we *do not* get along. In fact, I would sometimes liken her to my archenemy. At times, we are both stubborn and hotheaded. But she's a risk-taker, and no one can deny her extreme bravery.

My mother didn't graduate high school. Instead, she fled from abusive alcoholic parents, moving across the country when she was 16 years old. On her own, she made ends meet until she was in her late twenties. Then she returned home to take care of her mother and sister. She enrolled in a GED program, followed by nursing school, and then eventually, dental school. She also graduated top of her class as a "late learner" while pregnant with me. She opened her own practice shortly after I was born and was a business owner until she had a grade-five aneurysm three years ago.

She was in a catatonic state for two months, until she pulled through a grueling six months of inpatient therapy, and then another year of outpatient therapy. By any expectations of her treating physicians, she should have been brain dead upon arrival at the hospital... and then in a permanent coma after two weeks of being unresponsive... and then a vegetable after she started to respond... and so on. Except she wasn't. That stubborn New Yorker that is my mother pulled all the way through and is now hardly distinguishable from the woman pre-stroke.

Let me digress and say we still have a strained relationship, no matter how hard we try to repair things. However, she is undeniably the source of my bravery. That woman fought against all odds, and I never expected anything less from myself.

So, I dedicate this story to my mother; the hard-headed woman who never made life easy, but who taught me to live life *despite* ease, and taught me to live it with grace. This is why I know that all women are brave. We are born brave, as are men. We just need to change our definition of bravery to include the feminine connotation. We need to foster bravery in girls from a young age and never say you can be sweet *or* brave. You are sweet *and* brave. You are smart *and* brave. You are soft *and* brave.

I urge all ladies to be brave. Travel the road less taken. Take risks. Trust yourself. There's a whole world waiting to see where your bravery can take you. Go show them what you've got!

**For me to use this word seems almost silly, because I am no more or less brave than any other woman I have met or have yet to meet. But I've never lost my bravery and over time, have learned how to tap into it. I hope my story can inspire women to remember that risk is intrinsic to womanhood.

jen.scherb@gmail.com

PINKK on POINT: Kindness is vulnerable and strong. Be vulnerable. Be strong. Be kind. That is truly brave.

RESILIENCE
BY SHARLENE JONES

I want to be free to write a love story. Instead, I'm at a trailhead, recalling how to use what I learned in middle school cross-country track to counter the pain I feel from a story which predates my birth by more than 20 years. I was recently at a writer's conference where I read a story written by a very successful, published white author's perspective. It was a story he wrote about what he saw as a romance of his with a black woman in the 1950s. Tragically, her life was cut short by her violent murder—a murder in which she was beaten beyond recognition.

He described it fondly as a romance, while I recognized it as sexual assault, exploitation, and dehumanization. I was a cop in California. It's not like I haven't seen crime scenes or am overreacting to a murder. I'm black. I'm female. I'm the mother of three daughters, including one in college.

I can't unhear or unread his story. Now it is forever woven into the fabric of the heavy shroud passed down to me by my ancestors. So, I find myself facing a trailhead to choose a path so I can run through the pain—a pain which persists at the intersection of white privilege and my most basic human need to exist and thrive. I just want to write a love story, but before I can, I have work to do.

This is where that pain has taken me, back to middle school, back to my first lesson, the one I need to get through what I just experienced.

Coach Darling gave me my first lesson in resilience at Tioga Middle School. He was the cross-country coach, a team my single mother compelled me to join to keep me occupied during the time between school letting out and when she got home from work. I wasn't an athlete, though; add to that the fact that we were poor, and that combination meant my slightly overweight body ran in $5.00 canvas Keds, which had nowhere near the support of proper running shoes.

I got excruciating shin splints during every practice and always came in last. Coach Darling never let me stop running, even though he knew the flimsy shoes were the main reason for my pain. He would see me slowing down, pain clearly projected onto my face. I know he also observed that I ran with an awkward gait to accommodate the relentless stabbing assault to my shins every time I took a step.

He'd sprint up to me, aligning his towering six-foot-plus body right next to mine. He did this not to give me encouragement, but would instead spit out threats, to keep me going. In hindsight I can laugh, but at the moment, the fear of what he might do to me if I stopped outweighed the pain I was enduring by continuing to run, so I'd keep going.

His threats weren't so terrible, though. He mostly yelled, "You *better* keep running!" His accentuation of "better" carried implications of a harsh penalty for noncompliance. Quite curiously, he also yelled, "Run through the pain!" which suggested there was a certain relief in sight if I kept progressing despite the pain. So, I'd keep running. At some point, my legs would go numb and then they'd feel normal again. This little discovery didn't turn me into a star athlete. I conquered my legs, but still had to figure out my breathing, overall body mechanics and endurance. However, learning to run through the pain was, and continues to be, transformational in areas of my life that go beyond running.

Coach Darling ultimately had a heart-to-heart with me toward the end of the season where he admitted that he knew the shoes were a big part of my problem. He said he was so hard on me because "I needed to learn to run in the shoes I had." Since I had mastered running in those crappy shoes, he surprised me with a pair of new proper running shoes and gave them to me for the final meet.

So, as I faced the trailhead to choose a route, I looked for the stretch, and at the metaphorical "shoes I had"—the options and choices that would help me run through the pain I was feeling. A choice that would land me in the uncomfortable space between what I knew I could accomplish on present physical reserves, and what I had to accomplish over and above that comfort zone. I needed to get in the space where infinite mental capacity kicks in and takes over from finite physical resources.

I thought about Coach Darling, and those $5.00 Keds. I remembered what I had learned from that experience but needed something more. So, while other attendees were writing, napping, or exploring, I went for a hike on a nearby trail.

I decided on that particular trail because I knew that it would stretch my ability to complete it before the sunset. I knew darkness would raise the stakes. I didn't have a headlamp; the area was unfamiliar; nobody knew where I'd gone. Running with my service dog Titan would potentially attract coyotes at dusk, and the run could trigger a medical condition I have—exercise induced anaphylaxis (EIA). EIA is a condition that sometimes kicks in when I exercise. If untreated, it can kill. The potential of it sending me into anaphylactic shock alone on a dark trail loomed large. I set myself up to not have the luxury of choosing to fail. Good choice? Smart choice? I don't know. It was my choice.

I was training for resilience, not endurance. In the face of the visceral pain from the "romance" I'd just read, and the writer's justification of his point of view, I needed to remind myself to summon forth the fierce spirit that resides at my core. I needed to run through the pain to know that all I'll ever need to survive and thrive is contained neatly within me, and that one day, I'll be free to write a love story which honors the voices of my people.

Resilience is what has always gotten me through—it's what I coach and teach other women of color to get them through as well. It's powerful, it's personal, and it's my favorite word because it's my superpower. It's more than powerful. It's kind—because it is something we do for ourselves. It belongs in every woman's tool bag.

justjones11@gmail.com

PINKK on POINT: Resilience leads to kindness and to the untold love story we all want to read.

DRIVER
BY CLAIRE VAN NESS

Some would say I'm a driver—strong and practical, focused and funny. Like many people, it all began with my family and their story. It starts with an immigrant story like many others at the turn of the century. It is the story of my grandmother Jean, the oldest girl in a family of 11 children in Northern Ireland. My grandmother was smart and excelled in school but having to take care of younger siblings and work the farm for her family held her back from achieving her full potential. Because of this grueling schedule for a young student, she said she'd feel embarrassed that she was often unprepared for lessons the next day at school. She ended up with only a sixth-grade education.

Being so poor in Ireland, whenever her mother would get pregnant, Jean would ask, "Why do we keep having babies when we don't have enough to feed the ones we have?" Her days were an endless routine of chores on the farm. As she described them, I remember her reciting her chores like a sing/song–like so many Irish songs and verses. She said, "All day I'd be milking cows, feeding chickens, washing clothes, baking bread..." and so on.

As she grew, she had to take on the responsibility of the family's second farm, working as her mom did on the main farm. More work and responsibility with little time for herself. She told me that as a kid, she and her brother would say, "Let's run far away so we don't hear ma calling after us."

In the early 1900s, if you were still unmarried by age 30, they considered you an old maid. Jean was unmarried, working hard day in, day out. One day, she found a smidgeon of time to attend a church social. That is where she met Sammy. They began to date, and Sammy soon told her he was planning to travel to America for a better life. He asked Jean to join him. The plan was, he would set out first, get employment and then send her money to come over.

For poor Irish immigrants, coming to America was not a journey for the faint of heart. My grandmother told me many Irish men back then left for America, promising to send money back for passage for their girlfriends. Instead, several found wives in America, leaving their girlfriends behind. Sammy was different. He found a job and although it took several years, he sent money back to Ireland so that Jean could come. One day she asked her mother, "Should I go with Sammy?"

Her loving mother responded, "Yes, you should go to America in hopes of a better life. After all, what's the best you could hope for here? Being the oldest sister working on a farm, tending to your brother's kids…? Go, Jeannie, go!" She selflessly offered this advice, knowing she'd never see her daughter again in her lifetime.

So, my grandmother set sail for America on a boat filled with immigrants. She discovered she was prone to seasickness and was ill the entire voyage. When they finally reunited in the U.S., they got married and Sammy continued working at the Sherwin Williams Paint factory in Chicago. He and Jeannie settled into a small apartment in Roseland, surrounded by many Irish families.

Jean had been experiencing terrible pain during her monthly menstruation cycle. She would say that in the old country, they would state matter-of-factly, "Oh, it's just 'woman's pain.'" But after months of watching his wife suffer, one day Sammy took her to a doctor in Chicago. She was rushed into surgery after they discovered a five-pound tumor in her womb, which doctors removed.

Right after she recovered, Jean had her one and only child, my mother, Ann. Sammy and Jeannie were so happy to be parents. It seemed things were looking up. A short time later their luck would change again. At the factory, a large conveyor belt broke and struck Sammy. He became paralyzed from the waist down, confining him to a wheelchair the rest of his life. Fearing dismissal, Sammy didn't report the accident initially, so the company provided no insurance for the accident. As a result, Jeannie was forced to find work quickly. With only a 6th grade education, she became housekeeper to a wealthy family. The good news was that they gave her hand-me-down clothes from their girls, and these became Ann's school clothes.

As my mom was growing up, many supportive Irish families pitched in to help them. In fact, my dad told me much later that the neighborhood threw several fundraisers for the family after Sammy's accident.

Ann grew up happy in her neighborhood, even though the family had very little. Mom's family did not have hot running water. Hot water came from kettles on the stove. She went to Scanlan School in the city and her childhood sweetheart, Fred, rode her on his bike the long way home, even though she lived across the street from the school.

Ann loved to sing and shared this talent with her father, who would sing old Irish songs with her. She would sit on his lap and sing with him in his wheelchair. When Ann was 17, Sammy died. Jeannie was getting older and had trouble with her joints from doing floors the many years she was a housekeeper.

Ann also excelled in school and advanced up a grade ahead of her peers. She did so well that after high school, her church offered her a college scholarship. But she declined the scholarship and went to work for the phone company to help support her mom.

After her childhood friend Fred returned from WWII, he saw a familiar gabardine skirt on a familiar girl walking in front of him. Ann married Fred, the nicest guy who not only married her, but brought along her mom Jeannie, who would live with them for the rest of her life.

For me, this is a story of family, of sacrifice, history and strength; of choices and how our circumstances can change in a moment and how to make the most of what we have. It is a story of how to see opportunity in every challenge and reach for something more. It is the story of my family, and it gives me perspective when challenges arise in my own life. Remembering my grandmother's courageous journey keeps me thankful and faithful amid real challenges. It gives me a sense of strength and perspective.

PINKK on POINT: If you make the most of what you have then kindness and families will prevail.

AMPLIFY
BY SAUDIA DAVIS

I use the word "amplify" to explain my ability to help others, be it an individual, business or in one case, a building. Amplifying is all about increasing the abilities or success of others.

From the time I was seven, I remember constantly saying to other kids, "Hi. My name is Saudia. What's your name?"

I have always been curious about other people and their motivation. To this date, I ask adults, "What do you do during your day? What grabs your attention? What do you want most out of life?"

While I was curious, I was also quite an advocate for my friends. As a result, the bullies at my school would regularly gather their posse and come after me. My strategy brain kicks in like a matrix with constant flowing streams of information, cool new ideas, and people whom I know might be good collaborators for any of these insights. The potential success formula for what it would take to make these ideas work come flowing in, too!

Then new questions start spinning forth: Who do I know who can push these ideas even further? What might they know? What next steps do I need to accelerate the success of these ideas—to at least move to the next level?

Somewhere in all these blasts of awesome thoughts, I realize that this is that extra value I bring to the table in my relationships and work. I'm the "Amplifier!"

Maybe because I'm a survivor of bullying. I love and am not ashamed to admit that I enjoy the feeling I get when other people share with me their gratefulness for taking time, really listening to their needs, and then digging deep into my heart, soul, and mind to offer them support quickly and as richly as possible. I'm like a proud Momma to others, from children to grown-ups, to companies, and organizations of all sizes!

I love amplifying—especially for nonprofits like the school in one of Chicago's at-risk communities where I helped rebuild a fantastic 1,000 seat theatre. But now my challenge is to figure out how to *amplify* my own life.

How do I turn my amplification inward? I've been so busy "giving" to others I am feeling depleted. Generally speaking, women give too much. Right? We have a tremendously strong nature-nurture gene. But what happens when we give so much we feel like we've run out of steam to help ourselves? We are so strong in helping others—now it's time we do the same for us!

Shine your inner light and turn your attention and intentions within. That's not being selfish. Call me selfish if you want... but I call it "self-sustaining" or "self-preservation." In order to power up, we must power down into our core!

redwoodcovefilms@gmail.com

PINKK on POINT: Give back. Get back and thereby amplify kindness.

NO
BY PAT CHEEKS, RN, PMHCNS-BC

*"Half of the troubles of this life can be traced to saying
yes too quickly, and not saying no soon enough."*
~ Josh Billings

My heart went out to the woman in front of me in line at a major bookstore. The clerk was insistent on selling her a book card membership, a $25 annual fee. She clearly and confidently said, "No thanks, not today." But that fed the fuel. Saying no to that clerk was like waving a red flag in front of a bull. He said, "Really?" in an arrogant tone that implied she was crazy to pass up such a great deal. It rattled her. She thought for a moment, then said, "No, no, I really don't want a card today." I think everyone in line was silently rooting for her, even though the next few exchanges showed her appear to weaken and almost cave to his insistence.

She even looked in her wallet briefly for support. Despite her obvious discomfort, he persisted. I thought I saw her about to buckle in and buy a card; then she straightened her shoulders, stood up and said, strongly and while looking him in the eye.

"No, I really don't want one." The clerk looked disgusted. He said, "Well, okay, it's your loss," in a tone that implied she was crazy or at least stupid for turning down his offer. She looked at him and calmly said, "I suppose it is." She took her bags, her purchase and her dignity and left.

A woman behind me cheered, "Go girl!" and yet, when I stepped up to buy my books the clerk began again with his sales pitch. "Do you want to buy a book card today?" "No, thank you. I don't want to buy a book card today," I said firmly, looking him in the eye. I felt both intimidated and empowered after watching the woman before me. He taunted, "Are you sure?"

He launched into the same scripted aggression he had tried on the woman in front of me. I was surprised. Like the woman in front of me, I had been very clear about what I wanted - or rather didn't want. I said no in a very strong, matter-of-fact way, and still he persisted.

I might have caved and bought a card myself if I hadn't witnessed the slender young woman in front of me stand her ground. He looked at me and at the long line of customers behind me, obviously upset with the exchange. Then he let it drop. I left feeling both nervous, excited, scared, and a bit miffed.

What is it about the word "no," that makes it hard for people to hear, but harder for people to say and to stand by it?

I've worked with many sexual assault survivors over the years, many of whom struggled with the fact they did say "no." Yet their date ignored them. Had they not said it strongly enough? Were they not clear? Did they say no in a way that implied yes?

Watching and experiencing this conversation with the store clerk reminded me how powerful and necessary it is to learn to say and enforce our "No" to friends. While it might seem like a cruel, harsh, or blunt word to be passionate about I believe it's the strongest, yet kindest word in the English language. I coach a variety of men and women through all of life's transitions, and at the core of each transition is that word "no." It's the word that allows us to set boundaries. It's the word that protects our hearts, our time, our energy. Yet, it's hard to say "No"—especially to family and friends.

None of us want to be the bad guy. We don't want to disappoint those around us. We want to please those we love, or even work with. Many of us have grown up believing it's bad, wrong, or negative to say "no" to any request, reasonable or not. But it's not.

"No" is the perfect answer when enforcing or communicating our boundaries. "No" helps us keep the peace.

"No" lets others know what they can expect from us, and it frees us to do what we need to do for ourselves. Different people say "no" in different ways, all of them are effective, but some work better than others, depending on your personality, your confidence levels, your assertiveness or your boundaries.

What I have learned about this magical word is that when used with passion, feeling, intent and purpose, it works. As I say in my book, *How to Say No Without Feeling*

Guilty, Horrible, Selfish, Mean or Bad, "No," is a complete sentence. We don't need to explain, although we can choose to. We don't need to elaborate, and I encourage that. I also say:

Don't be afraid to repeat yourself. If you're not used to saying no, you can expect some pushback from the friends and family who aren't used to hearing you say no. Just because a person doesn't listen the first time doesn't mean they won't listen to the third or fourth time you say it—especially if you communicate consequences for not listening.

Practice makes perfect. The most important thing about saying no is practicing it. Have you ever raised, or been around a two-year-old? In a healthy family when they discover the word "No," they say it every chance they get — even to things they really want, like ice cream, or a trip to the park. They are fascinated by the word, and they practice saying it. If the adults around them listen and honor their "no," even if it's nonsensical, the child will integrate his/her awareness and skill into their developing personality. Learning how, when, and where to say no at a young age is invaluable, but it's a word that can be learned at any age.

Saying no to others, even family, friends and those we love, is not being selfish or mean. One of the myths I often have to dispel is that even when we do say no, and have a right to say no, that some people aren't going to be very happy with us. They will try to manipulate, guilt, shame, or intimidate us into changing our minds. It's up to us to decide when and where it's in our best interest to keep saying no or to say yes.

Understanding that even though we have a right to say no, and a right not to give-in to another's demands, the process and the interaction can be uncomfortable, scary and frightening. Say it anyway. You can love someone and still say no.

Good boundaries are healthy boundaries. How do you respond when someone tells you no? Do you feel hurt, or offended, or do you accept it and find someone else to ask a favor of? Saying no is the core of any good boundary. It helps us identify our limits and tells others how we want and expect to be treated and what the consequence of not respecting our boundary will mean.

I have several clients who have learned to say, "I can't hear you when you raise your voice when we're talking. Please lower your voice or this conversation is over until we can speak in normal tones." If their spouse or boss continues to speak loudly, or yell, they say, "This conversation is over, I'm walking away now," and then walk away." They have learned to ask for what they need, which is not to be yelled at. When they walk away it sends a message but does so in a respectful way. They have told the offender what they want and have demonstrated that they respect themselves enough to hold out for the treatment they deserve.

Other phrases we practice saying:

- "It's not possible for me right now. In fact, it's impossible given my schedule."
- "Last time/last year when I did this, it was great, but I am not available this year."
- "Thank you for asking, but I'm happy with my current phone/insurance/healthcare/cable/television company, so no thank you."

When we understand that saying no is a kindness that protects everyone involved, we begin to enjoy saying it, not because it frees us up from all the unwanted favors, tasks, and requests we don't want to do, but because it frees us up *to do* the things we truly want to do.

https://naturaltransitions.com

Pat@PatCheeks.com

PINKK on POINT: When we say no it can open the floodgates to more kindness we all deserve. There is no one written sales pitch for kindness.

EMPOWERING
BY KJ VAN

My former boss and good friend, John, is the foundation for my word Empowering. John hired me for a marketing position at Englewood Electric in 1993 when I was looking to move to Chicago and start my next chapter of work and life. John not only taught me many things about business and life, he also enabled me to meet my husband, the controller at Englewood Electric.

So how did John empower me? He helped me prepare for meetings with vendors, showing me the importance of making the numbers match, setting a goal for the meeting, preparing slides and telling the story.

He also advised me on the importance of having P&L (Profit and Loss) responsibility. When he first talked about me taking over at P&L, I told him, "But I just enjoy marketing." His reply sticks with me today: "Kathy Jo, even in marketing, you need and want to have accountability to the bottom line because if you don't, you're dispensable."

He showed me, by example, how you get back so much more with kindness and a calm demeanor than through strong-arming. Many years later, his reputation continues as a well-respected, fair and thoughtful leader in the industry.

He gave me opportunities along with the backing and support to succeed. After I mastered one product category, he gave me more. Then he gave me the opportunity to manage other people. He coached me through recruiting and developing people and through letting some go.

When WESCO acquired Englewood Electric, John's encouragement gave me the confidence to pursue and tackle new opportunities. And when he left the company, he continued to be my mentor. I'd occasionally call to ask for his advice or perspective. But he was also a virtual mentor, giving me the inspiration to reflect on "What would John do?" in many moments of life and career.

When Southwire took over Coleman Cable (the company I worked for from 2000 to 2014), one of my first calls was to John. You see, Southwire was a competitor of Coleman... we had always called them "the evil empire." I wasn't sure I wanted to join this organization or just move on to another company. So, I called John. He had great words of wisdom as he calmly said, "Kathy Jo, Southwire is good people. You should give them a chance." So, I did, and it turned out to be a great adventure, helping me continue to grow and learn as a leader and as a person.

Then, in 2017, I made a personal decision to retire from Southwire. It was a choice between continuing to spend more time in Carrollton working versus spending time with my husband and family in the city I moved to 24 years earlier.

Everyone's definition of retirement is different. When I began my journey to define my version of retirement, I wanted a way to stay connected and give back. As I reflected on my career, I found I had several amazing mentors (John included) who encouraged me, challenged me, supported me and helped me become the person I am today. But I lucked into it. If I had known then what I know now, I would have been much more intentional and deliberate in finding and building mentoring relationships.

So began my mission to enable and empower individuals at all levels of their career to understand the value of mentoring. But it's more than just understanding, I developed a four-step process that helps individuals take a very deliberate and intentional approach to finding a mentor and then building a mentoring relationship. I teach this process through workshops, an online video series, and by helping organizations develop, launch, and implement a mentoring program uniquely suited to their culture and needs.

It was so rewarding to see the mentoring pilot come to life with PINKK. Only a few weeks into the pilot, I'm already hearing phenomenal feedback on the journey and experience of the mentors and mentees.

At about the same time that we launched the PINKK Mentoring Pilot, I also launched the E2E Summit mentoring pilot for nine contractors matched with nine hand-selected mentors. It's amazing to feel the energy from these guys empowered through the benefit of mentoring.

When I was honored to receive the NAED Women in Industry Trailblazer award in 2018, I used my acceptance speech and on-line/magazine article as an opportunity to share three messages with individuals (men and women) in the industry:

1. **Enjoy the journey**. I was often so busy focusing on the next big project or promotion that I forgot to pause and just enjoy all the wonderful opportunities and people that I met.

2. **Check your woman card**. The electrical industry, like many other industries, has very few women. It's growing, but still has a long way to go to become diverse. My advice to women (and minorities) is to not go into a conversation as a "woman" in the industry (sometimes with that little chip on our shoulder or with "a woe is me" attitude). Instead, just enter the conversation as a "member" of the industry. It's amazing how the change in perspective shifts the conversation.

3. **Find a mentor**... or two... or even ten. They are invaluable.

I'm the "busiest retired person" that my husband knows. And I guess that's okay because I'm fortunate to be doing something that I love to do. My biggest reward is the feedback I receive from the people I have successfully empowered:

"Truly adoring this process." (Mentee in a pilot mentoring program)

"The best part of this was that you didn't just talk about mentoring in an abstract way, you gave specific steps and "how-to" advice." (Participant in Mentoring workshop)

"KJ is strong, smart, articulate, with a true generosity of spirit. So glad our paths crossed." (Friend and peer mentor)

kjvann@gmail.com

PINKK on POINT: Kindness is mentoring and empowering. Try it.

FORWARD
BY NANCY REID

I was born and raised in Detroit. Back in the day, Detroit was a growing, prosperous city. As a kid, it was a wonderful time. Our neighborhood was full of children, and in the summertime, we played for hours on end. It was a wonderful time and a wonderful memory.

My dad grew up on a farm outside of Paducah, Kentucky. My mother, on a small farm in the Upper Peninsula of Michigan. Both wanted a better life, and both moved to Detroit. That's how they met. My dad came up from the south, like many men did, to get a job with one of the big car companies. My mom left the UP to find life in a big city. My dad got a job at Ford Motor Company and worked there for a couple of years. The history of layoffs at the big car companies goes back to the early beginnings. My dad and his brother got laid off at the same time.

They had to figure out what was next. How to support their families. They both were extremely capable and had wonderful mechanical minds. They thought about how they could start their own business. They met a man who owned a gas station and was ready to retire. My dad and his brother made a deal with the owner. "If you teach us how to fix cars and run a business, we'll buy the gas station." It worked.

He trained both my dad and my uncle. It was a Sunoco Gas Station. The brothers became partners. My uncle died in an unfortunate car accident, making Dad the sole proprietor. He ran that gas station for 30 years. He really provided us with everything we could ask for. He was a great inspiration and one of the hardest working people I have ever met in my life. I'm sure that's where I got my entrepreneurial spirit!

My mother was a great inspiration, too. She was a stay-at-home mom and cared for our every need. From the moment we got up in the morning until she tucked us in at night, she was there for us. My mom was so wonderful and helpful in more ways once I started high school. She would help me rehearse my lines for the current school play. She was a Cub Scout Leader for my two brothers and the Girl Scout leader for my troop. I joke that selling Girl Scout cookies was my first sales job!

FORWARD

I attended grammar school one block from my house—kindergarten through 9th grade. Again, a delightful experience. A time to grow and time to make friends. Lots of friends. Now it was time to transfer to high school.

FORWARD

My 9th grade counselor recommended me to be our student council representative. This was a dream come true because it exposed me to a wide variety of kids, different grades (sophomores, juniors and seniors) and different ethnicities. In the 11th grade I joined the drama club. Wow! What a growing experience. And talk about a great confidence builder. Being on stage, in front of a whole auditorium filled with my high-school peers made me feel extra special. And when you feel extra special, it creates a sense of belonging and support. You feel like you can compete and overcome anything. My confidence builder!!

FORWARD

During high school I met a really cute, personable guy. We started to date. We fell madly in love. Against my parents' wishes (they begged me not to do it) we married. It was a huge mistake. After 18 months, I realized this wasn't what I wanted. I was still so young. I decided to end it. It was hard, but really what I needed to do.

My parents had done their best to convince me not to marry because I was so young. Yet, despite their opposition to the union, they supported me all the way through ending my marriage. They were great parents.

Because of my early decisions, I didn't start college until I was 21 years old. I first attended a community college in a suburb of Detroit, and one year later transferred to Eastern Michigan University. I met a guy from the University of Michigan, and we dated for approximately two years. Again, it was a great experience as I met a lot of new people and had the wonderful experience of college life in Ann Arbor and Ypsilanti, Michigan.

I consider myself a late bloomer. I didn't really find my way until I was about 28 years old. That's the year I moved to Chicago from Detroit. That's when life really began.

FORWARD

Back to post college. I was living in Ann Arbor, Michigan, working at a prestigious country club. A member there hired me to be a greeter at their television syndication company suite in Miami for a big television conference (NATPE, National Association of Television Producers & Executives). Our job was to welcome the TV station executives as they entered the suite and share information about the company until one of the syndication executives was available to talk about their fall lineup. After three days, the conference was over. The "man in charge" approached me and said, "You're a natural salesperson." He said he'd like to help me pursue a career in sales if I was interested. That's the day this man became my mentor and sponsor. He changed my life forever. What an incredible gift he gave me.

FORWARD

From there he offered me a job at a TV production studio and videotape duplication company with offices in Ann

Arbor. Eighteen months later, the same man recommended me to a BIG videotape editing company in Chicago. They specialized in TV commercials, corporate communications, and basically any programming that needed a creative editor. I spent the next 20 years being offered a variety of sales and management positions at four different videotape production and post-production companies.

Eventually, I became one of the few women V.P. and general managers in the Chicago production post/production community. During this time, I married my former husband, who was also in the business. We worked together on a variety of projects. He also became one of my biggest clients. Things changed between us and eventually we split. A few years before our split, I also left the video production world to pursue a job in children's book publishing. That lasted for about five years and was a great experience. Next, I was recruited to return to the video production world - this time to work as an independent business development representative. I've been doing that ever since.

A couple years after my marriage ended, I met a wonderful man while attending a human development course. Over the course of the next two years, we fell in love and got engaged. He was an architect for many years in Chicago. When the crash hit in 2008-2009, about half of the architects in Chicago became unemployed, including my fiancé. It really took a toll on him. He went back to work briefly for a boutique architectural firm in 2013. That transition period was overwhelming for him. He became so depressed and unable to cope that he ended his life on Tuesday, December 31st, 2013. I knew he had been feeling overwhelmed, but when it's someone close to you, you never think suicide. It was heartbreaking and still is a devastating loss.

I will always cherish our time together. Our relationship was one I'll never forget and always cherish. And one I'll never get over. But you must move **FORWARD** and keep going. And so, I do. There's a poem I often refer to written by an artist by the name of *Brian Andreas*. "There are days I drop words of comfort on myself like falling rain & remember it is enough to be taken care of by myself."

I continue to work with a variety of companies/industries with their business development. I realized there are a lot of companies that need someone like myself to help them develop new clients and new business. That's what I'm good at. And I really enjoy sales/business development, working with creative people from various industries.

Work has always been grounding for me. Coming from an entrepreneurial father and hard-working stay-at-home mother, I knew I could be a rainmaker and take care of myself.

FORWARD!

I celebrate the good times and the sad times. My former spouse and I have become friends and spend some enjoyable times together. So, my marriage has a happy ending.

I have a great family and a group of friends that all help me keep moving **FORWARD.** My two brothers Ken and Phil have and continue to be supportive. Even though they're in the Detroit area, we keep our strong bond as a family. My former husband is also very supportive. And like I said, I have a wonderful group of friends. I am so fortunate!! **FORWARD** is my word.

Nancylreid@earthlink.net

PINKK on POINT: Move forward with kindness and love. It can change your world and those that you love.

RECKONING
BY DANIELLE SWANSON

A number of years ago I was in the throes of wedding planning. My fiancée and I were planning to get married outside of the state in which we lived (D.C.), outside of either of our home states (Illinois and California), and instead we decided to get married in a state in which we had four total family members - two from each side. A total "neutral state" by design.

I am a planner and organizer at heart, plus a crafter and doer and an "I can do it all myself-er." Add to it that we made one single visit to the state a year before the big day in order to meet with potential vendors, and subsequently did all remaining planning by internet and phone (with most of the signage and paper goods done by myself)... let's just say I didn't make it easy on us.

In one of the hundreds of blogs I visited during those planning days, I came across a bit of advice I have not yet forgotten. It's changed my perspective and the way I handle new situations. It's short, simple, easy to remember, and something I keep in my back pocket as a mantra that I've used handfuls of times since I first read it.

"You are not the first person to _____."

In the particular blog I read, it was "You are the not the first person to get married."

Bam. It hit me like cold water in the face. I generally am not self-centered, but when it comes to wedding planning, something happens to you. Something takes control of you and says, "Everyone needs to do what I want, how I want it, when I want it, and if it's not right, they must not love me." Or something to that drastic nature.

It's what bridezillas are made of. And while I was no-where near a bridezilla (not just by my own account, I swear), in my own head I had some feelings that a nice person just shouldn't have. Like "this is MY wedding, why aren't they doing things special for me?" "This is MY wedding, why isn't this vendor giving me a discount?" "This is MY wedding, why is everyone in my life not more interested?"

For instance, something that threw a wrench in the plans happened with our chosen wedding photographer. I found his website online and knew he was expensive, but thought he was kind of a genius in his style. We met with him when we did our "site visit," along with about 5 other wedding photographers, but in my mind, I was set on him.

My husband, not so much. He thought the photographer had a bit of an ego. But we went with him because he was who I wanted. Because I do photography myself, includ-ing photo retouching and photo books, we made it clear to everyone we met with that all we needed was their tal-ent in taking the photos and delivering the files to us, and I would do the rest.

Four months later, just after the first of the year, he called me to let me know there was another couple who wanted to book the same date, but they wanted a huge package. More expensive photography. Photobooks. The works. He explained to me that he wanted to switch us to his second photographer so he could book this other couple, as if this was done all the time and totally normal to tell a bride-to-be who specifically booked a certain photographer that someone else was going to shoot the wedding.

It took me a very long week to find someone else to shoot the wedding, all while keeping this other photographer strung along. We didn't want him to do the wedding anymore knowing he would not be thrilled to be missing out on a lot more money, nor did we want him anymore knowing money was a major motivator, but we also couldn't cut the ties until we had someone else to take his spot.

That was nerve-wracking, very frustrating, and one of the most difficult parts of our wedding planning. Truly, none of this matters now, especially given what some other couples experience during their planning, but at the time it seemed like a major deal.

But again. "You are not the first" rang true.

Once I got that earworm inside my head, it changed the way I thought about things.

They were right. I wasn't the first person to ever get married. Once I thought about that, I thought about the thousands of other weddings happening the same day as ours.

I thought about the thousands of other weddings that my vendors had worked on before ours. The thousands of weddings they would do after ours, ours being a single (awesome) blip on the radar. I thought of the thousands of other weddings that our friends and family had attended before ours. Boy, does that give you something to think about.

It helped me relax. People weren't going to expect everything to be perfect. One of the key points to know when planning a wedding is that something will ALWAYS go wrong. It's just how it is. But the important thing is how you react to it. So as long as our guests had a good time (which they did), and as long as we were married once the day was over (which we were), that's all that mattered.

Because this piece of advice was so useful to me, I've carried it with me during other extremely stressful times, like during my first pregnancy. And, mind you, that pregnancy was easy. So easy. Like almost textbook normal. (Almost. Because like weddings, something always is a little different from what you expect during pregnancy.) But pregnancy and the thought of a baby was so new to me that it freaked me out. Remembering how many millions of women before me have given birth kept me grounded and sane.

During pregnancy number two, when we learned we were having a son after having a daughter, I was anxious, paranoid, and nervous about how to raise a son, or rather how to raise him "properly." I kept thinking about how we've raised our daughter rather successfully but about how different a boy would be. I had to remember my handfuls of friends who had a daughter first and then a son, and somehow, they've managed. Somehow the world keeps turning. And somehow, we too, made it through because we are not the first to have two children of different genders.

Sure, having two children is difficult. Managing two individual little humans with their own little minds and personalities is difficult. As everyone has said, "No child is the same." What your first one did, your second will not. How your first one acted, your second will not. If that isn't true, then I don't know what is. What I do know is every day I'm doing my best to maneuver life with beautiful, strong souls who love me but who also love to push my buttons, and it will continue this way for probably the rest of my life. But it's ok, because I'm trying to make it day by day just like most everyone else.

And, I am not the first.

It's comforting in a way. I'm not forging any new pathways. I'm following deep entrenched roadways. In my own way, but still following. There are still those before me who can give me advice and love and support. And they will. No doubt about that.

I am not the first.

PINKK on POINT: Kindness means recognizing that you are not the first, probably ever; and if you really are the first then set the example of kindness for the rest of us.

HUNGER
BY ANNE BORG

I grew up in Winnipeg, Manitoba, Canada in a very happy, traditional family. My passion in life was reading and my parents indulged me in every way to support that, including letting me off the hook for chores when I had my nose in a book. The outside world didn't exist for me while I was engaged in other worlds and other people's insights.

Despite my father's hope that I would become a writer, I went to business school and worked at amazing companies like Procter & Gamble and Frito-Lay before going to a little known, third-party logistics company. I was in charge of Business Development in the Americas (It's NOT Sales!!) and we grew the Americas Division from $160M to over $1 billion in 9 years.

I did well, because I've been blessed with some smarts. I am not afraid to lead, and I enjoy meeting new people. I loved my team and my job, but they let me go when the UK parent company pared down the America's management team to sell the company to its largest competitor. After that, I ran a small company and began consulting for a U.S. company, so my husband and I relocated to Chicago from Toronto. A few years later, we started a business in the cabinetry sales/kitchen design space—just as the 2008 recession hit.

As a result, while many of our friends are retiring and spending months in their second homes, I am not where I want to be financially—retirement is not an option and I need to reinvent myself.

As I look back, my life has been about "Acceptance," perhaps because I've been

surrounded by people who loved me despite my flaws. I love people and love that we are all so different; for all the commonalities of being human. I stay away from social media personally because of the pervasive hatred and lack of acceptance shown to people with differing perspectives.

I accept that everyone is imperfect, and that perfection for some is imperfection for others. There are always two sides to a story (or more) and I accept that people have a reason for believing and behaving as they do.

A pivotal moment in understanding this came in my midthirties when I read a book by Edward DeBono, a leader in the mechanics of how the human brain works, and the creator of the concept of "Lateral Thinking." His book, *Practical Thinking: Five Ways to be Wrong and Four Ways to be Right*, changed any tendencies I may have had to be judgmental of others.

I don't know if it made me more "accepting" of others or gave me an understanding of the way I was inherently, but it was a major influence in dealing with people going forward.

It helped me understand people better. It also made me a better manager, a better friend, a better team leader and mentor. Ironically, it even helped me fire employees more easily, people unsuited to the job they were in, knowing that I was setting them free to do something they would enjoy more.

I guess my one area of intolerance is people who let down the team—those who don't care about the impact of their actions or inactions on the people who depend on them.

"Acceptance" has really determined my life's path and the incredible jobs that have come my way. I did not seek them out. I was not looking for my amazing husband when he found me. I followed my high school boyfriend to business school instead of accepting an offer to go to the premier journalism school in Canada, and I've never regretted that path.

I am so grateful for my easy life, but at 60 years old, without the financial stability I had in my 40s when my husband and I were both in corporate jobs, I now realize that that Acceptance has had a cost.

I wake up happy every day. I don't know how to be hungry or scared about my future. I have never had to strive for survival. I have been so fortunate in where the currents in the river of my life have taken me, that I was unprepared to hit the rough waters in which I find myself now.

In every place I have landed, I always strived to make it better; to do the best job, to inspire people to care about a unifying goal and purpose, to help people discover their talents and to create a space where people are free to be themselves.

I have studied much about what makes people and businesses successful. Many, many successful people came out of lives fraught with pain and adversity and a resulting "Hunger" to change their lives–to escape and to grow. They had *purpose* in their lives.

How does someone with a full, happy life teach themselves to be HUNGRY? I am about to try.

PINKK on POINT: Acceptance and "hunger" can lead to kindness.

BREAKTHROUGH
BY ALISON EGAN

"Why are we all here? Because we're not all there!"
I'm Alison Egan, and that's my mantra for life.

I'm on a bus in the middle of rural County Cork in Ireland. It is the May Bank holiday weekend, and the sun is threatening to peek its head through the grey cloudy sky. The rain is slightly tapping against the windows as I look out over the faraway greener fields. At age 16, I'm on my way to an International Choral Competition with our choir teacher and all of my happy-go-lucky choir friends from the Sacred Heart School Choir, some of whom are my best friends to this day.

Those girls that were by my side undressed me, washed me, brushed my teeth, dressed me into my pajamas and hugged me tight in bed while I was shaking with anxiety attacks during my mental breakdown in Cork. For that, I will be forever grateful for their kindness, love, and empathy. I will cherish these girls forever. From there, my mum was called, and they rushed me to the Jonathan Swift Intensive Care unit of St. Patrick's Psychiatric hospital in Dublin where I stayed for two-and-a-half months of my young life.

How others see you is not important. How you see yourself is everything. When I was younger, I used to worry so much about what other people thought of me, if they liked me or if I was good enough. At one point, I believed nobody cared or loved me. I was going through a pretty rough time for a teenager. Dealing with parental divorce and upcoming state exams, the usual teenage angst piled on top of it all led me through a dark tunnel that seemed to go on forever.

It just happened to come to a head at that choral competition in Cork with my school choir friends. This tunnel was filled with demons from my head, shouting things like, "You are so ugly, nobody loves you. Even your dad wants nothing to do with you. You are too skinny, Lanky Ali!" they would taunt, shouting.

Those same words haunted me because the bullies from secondary school who would snigger as I passed them in the corridor had used them. Looking back on those times, I wish I could give myself a big hug, tell my younger self that everything will be okay and will work out just fine. It's so strange, because at the time you feel you're the only one going through shit. But in fact, everyone has his or her own shit to deal with and we are not alone. Those friends from my choir in Cork whose lives I thought were perfect were also far from it, and they dealt with their own mental health issues a little later on.

My funny mantra of a saying enabled me to get through my time of two-and-a-half months in St. Pat's psychiatric hospital. The friends I made while there would sit with me, and we'd have our tea and chats in the afternoon, reassuring ourselves with the saying, "Why are we all here?

Because we are not all *there*!" I suppose it made us feel more united and a little less crazy to know that we could laugh about not having our shit together! It made us look on the brighter side of life. I still say it from time to time if my husband and I are deep in the trenches of parenthood, having a rough day. It makes us both laugh and helps us to keep on trudging. I truly believe in finding humor in the darkest times is really the key to moving towards happiness.

So, back to my mental breakdown and what I learned during my time of healing. I figure it's not all that important to list all the reasons which may or may not have contributed to the breakdown, but rather, to list all the things I learned from it:

1. We are all deeply loved; If not by everyone, by our own family and inner circle and NEVER EVER doubt that. I will never forget the number of letters, cards, visits and little tokens I received from all of my family and friends, teachers and nuns at school during my time in hospital. One of my friends even wrote me a book of all our funny memories together! I still have them to this day, stored in an ornate box. I read them from time to time for encouragement. The nurses at the hospital thought it was my birthday with all the mail I was receiving. Here I was thinking nobody cared or loved me. It was not true.
2. Changing my focus from what others saw to caring about how I perceived myself gave me the

greatest freedom one could ask for in life. Once you are unafraid of the opinions of others, you are no longer a sheep, but a brave lion! I think this outlook gave me the courage to move to China after university. Most people who emigrated from Ireland took the paved path to Australia or America, but I chose the road less travelled. Now I'm not saying for one minute those that immigrated to those countries are less brave, but it's just that much easier because they actually speak English!

3. Speak kindly to yourself in the mirror and change the voice in your head to one of love and kindness. I've learned to replace the negative voice. Now all I hear in my head are the wise words of my caring grandmother. Some might resonate with you too. "Walk, don't run." ''Don't overdo it." "It's far better to be kind than right."
    ''People only treat you how you allow them to treat you." Her sayings need a whole other chapter!

4. Be comfortable with the entire spectrum of human emotion. It's okay to not be strong; it's okay to cry. It's okay to say, "I'm sick. I might need help and maybe go into a hospital." In fact, that in itself is a strength. Don't underestimate the power and freedom in opening up and telling someone close to you your problems and that you are feeling unwell.

For me, staying positive was not always easy when the whole world around me, at least as I knew it, was falling apart. I'm so grateful for my time in hospital now. I used to be embarrassed and ashamed to tell people, but now I think it was an amazing opportunity and was absolutely the right thing to do then. While there, I had access to the best psychiatrists Europe had to offer.

I think this strength came from my mum, who did not hide from anyone that I was mentally ill and in a psychiatric hospital. She is a very open and positive person. She doesn't "sweep anything under the carpet" or try to impress the neighbors. She is a very real person, which is one thing I really admire about her and try to follow suit.

5. Your life that you're living right now results from somebody else's dream for your life, so be grateful for all that you have. I remember when we had no money and no heating in our rented accommodation in Tullamore. My mum would bathe my little brothers in a basin by the fire, and they would moan to her, "Why do we have to have a bath in a basin by the fire?" My mum gave it a positive spin and told them how lucky they were, that none of their friends probably had an open fire in front of their bathtubs! Perspective.

6. Don't be a martyr. Be real to yourself and to others. Don't be putting on a brave face all the time.

Say no when you're not in the mood to see others and protect your time, but don't forget to say yes to the right things and experiences that nurture you.

My family time is my world. Spending time with my husband Jonny and son Harry are everything to me, but sometimes saying yes to the girls' night out or trips is so important. If you say no too many times, the invites will stop coming and you will feel left out, further enhancing your anxiety and feeding your negative voice of *Oh, I'm just the boring mum now, I've nothing exciting to talk about, nobody wants to hang out with me anymore.*

7. Laugh whenever you can! Laugh at yourself and make light of a situation when people are nasty to you, as we have no idea what space they are coming from. Frankly, with some people, you just can't win. Recently I've been dealing with certain neighbors who are so uptight about my kitty getting out on the loose. Every time we leave the house for work/school or just go out to collect the mail in the morning, our cat escapes like a bat out of hell and hits the streets! I've stopped running down the street after her in my underwear and nightdresses at this stage for fear of being put back in a mental institution!

8. Get out in nature! We cannot obtain the endorphins released while out in the woods or on the beach from a bottle or a pill. Go wild, you Nature's Child!

   Wild in Nature. I certainly did go wild in nature after a difficult breakup when my best friends and I lived in Beijing together. From camping at the Great Wall of China to cruising down the Yangtze River through the three Gorges; even climbing the dizzying heights of China's most dangerous mountain throughout the night to watch a sunrise. I will write a book on those invigorating adventures someday, albeit a censored version!

9. No matter how bad you feel, get up, wash, put on your war paint (make-up) and face the day! I remember in the early, dark days of motherhood I would look and feel like a zombie, but during my son's morning nap, I made sure to make time for me to shower, dress and put on some makeup. Even if it was just a bit of lip gloss and mascara! It really perked me up and made me feel a little bit better!

10. Don't compare yourself to others, only to yourself as you were yesterday. You are not the same person you were yesterday, or even the person you will become tomorrow. It might 'seem' like everyone else's life is better than your own through the lenses of social media, but it's all fake. It's all

just an illusion, a one-second snapshot of some-one's whole life not to be measured alongside your worth. It's just like the impression that I had on that bus in County Cork where I thought all my girlfriends had a way better and easier life than I had.

Today there is such an appalling number of suicides and mass shootings among young people. It just breaks my heart. If only someone had told them how beautiful they are, and how much they are loved; how much they have to offer the world and how much the world has in store for them. Told them enough until they truly believed it and knew they were never alone.

Don't suffer in silence. Go to your general practitioner. Talk to family and friends! Don't turn towards drugs, alcohol or other short-term fixes to numb the pain. Please see the beautiful light at the end of the dark tunnel, and just remember why we are all here... because we are not all *there*!

alison.oriordan@live.ie

PINKK on POINT: Seeking help is kind to one's soul. Giving help is kindness to others. Both make a difference in the world.

RESILIENCE
BY BECKY BLANTON

In 2006 I was living in a 1975 stripped out Chevy van in a Walmart parking lot in Denver, Colorado with my Rottweiler and my cat. I was homeless, terrified, and bordering on suicidal. I was working two jobs, about 60 hours a week, and could not find affordable housing. My father had just died, I'd quit my job as the editor of a small-town newspaper and had no idea what would happen next. I just trusted that God had a plan and everything would work out. It did.

Within two years I'd won a "Golden Presscard Award" in Tennessee for a writing project I did while living in my van. Three years after leaving Colorado (2009) I was on a world stage—speaking at TED Global in London at Oxford University, as the guest of Dan Pink (Former head speechwriter for Vice President Al Gore).

Those around me were surprised. I was not. Today I'm a ghostwriter for executives, Fortune 500 CEOs, and a variety of celebrities, speakers, and business owners. While the 18 months I spent living out of my van, all while working full-time, was difficult, often embarrassing, and frequently shame-inducing, it did not break me. I credit a lifelong trait of resilience for my success. Resilience is the capacity to recover quickly from difficulties. It's toughness, grit, or persistence in the face of challenges and trials. I've had it since I was a child. Both of my parents were brutally and physically abusive.

They both criticized, attacked, and tried to destroy any successes I had the minute they spotted them. As evil, hateful and useless as they both were, they had three traits I picked up on early on—resilience, a strong work ethic, and dogged perseverance. Both came from abusive backgrounds themselves. I assume they learned these traits to survive themselves. While I refused to adopt and practice their abusive tendencies, I embraced and received benefit from the work ethic, persistence in the face of challenges, and resilience.

The good news is, resilience can be learned. The bad news is, it takes time and a series of challenging difficulties to do so. For instance, if you want to learn patience, you do so by going through situations or experiencing people who cause you to be impatient. You learn patience by being challenged to become patient. You learn how to become a good listener by listening, and you learn to become resilient by bouncing back from adversity. That means to be resilient or tough, you have to be thrown into a situation, or lead a life that is constantly challenging you to rise above circumstances and find ways over, through, around, or under what is trying to hold you back or keep you down.

Looking back at my life, at a series of health crises (paralyzed at the waist at 20, then recovering and walking again after surgery), sexual assaults, job losses, PTSD, and a variety of work, life, and relationship challenges, I can see how my resilience grew. What I learned is that, as cliché as it sounds, you can do anything if you break it down into bite-sized chunks.

One bite at a time. An old vaudeville joke goes, "How do you eat an elephant?" The answer: "One bite at a time." St. Francis of Assisi phrased it more kindly: *Start by doing what's necessary; then do what's possible; and suddenly you are doing the impossible.* However you look at it, it's true. Somewhere along the line a Navy Seal friend told me the only way he got through SEAL training was to do just that—only he expounded on the concept, going against conventional wisdom to do so. While many people advise us to "focus on the goal," the SEALS teach their recruits to focus on the step at hand, not the end of the training, but on the training or event that is happening right then, right there.

"Think about hiking," he said. "Don't think about the summit. Think about getting from where you are now, to the next bend in the trail. Once you reach that bend, pick another landmark and focus on getting to it. Eventually, the next landmark will be the summit."

Visualize success, and when necessary, visualize failure to motivate yourself. See yourself experiencing your success. This differs from focusing on your goal. This is about feeling, smelling, tasting, and hearing what life will be like once you reach your goal.

Breathe. Breathing is everything. When you're stressed, scared, exhausted, fearful, tired or uncertain—breathe.

Inhale through your nose for four seconds. Hold the breath for another four seconds, then exhale for four seconds. Breath from your belly. It works.

Reframe the negative or the situation. Reframing situations is probably the most powerful technique I know. It involves finding the silver lining in every cloud, every illness, and every disaster. As I write this, I'm in week five of chronic laryngitis; I just had one foot surgery and need another; and I've had problems with diabetic neuropathy, pneumonia, and a variety of serious health issues. As an extrovert who relies on her voice for her business, it's been extremely challenging to go without a voice, and worse, to have to croak or whisper *sotto voce* my needs to doctors, waitresses, mechanics, merchants, and clients.

Being self-employed, when I don't work because of a variety of illnesses, I don't make money and can't pay bills! I've had to reframe these illnesses while being tested, prodded, and poked. Instead of focusing on what I can't do, I've worked to improve my listening and nonverbal skills. I've reframed these illnesses and am focusing on what I *can* do, not what I can't.

Practice gratitude. This is perhaps the most powerful of all the skills needed to be resilient—focus on what you have, not what you don't have. To this end I suggest keeping a gratitude journal and list 3 to 5 things you're grateful for every day. This doesn't just mean thanking God for an apartment, a car, and work. It means something new every day. What this does is really challenge you to see all the things you may take for granted.

For example: I'm thankful for things like a dentist who truly is pain free in his work on me. I'm thankful for two great loving, cuddle-addicted cats who know when I'm sick and sleep on me when I'm stressing. I'm grateful for a car that runs, food in the fridge, work, clients I adore, a comfortable bed, a door that locks. The things I didn't have while homeless are now huge luxuries to me—my own flushing toilet, a shower, heat and air-conditioning on demand.

Keep things in perspective. I once belonged to a women's group of about 15 women. We would meet and share the things going on in our lives that were challenging and then offer supportive feedback to each other. One week I listened to women describing the absolute worst things they were coping with. There was a woman whose toddler had just been diagnosed with cancer, another who lost her daughter to a DUI driver, and another whose husband had just been deployed overseas for his third military tour. Each woman in the group had a major life event - from a cheating husband to financial stresses that meant losing a home, serious health challenges and so on.

Then Jean spoke up. She was "devastated" (her word) by the fact her daughter and son-in-law had refused her gift of the family's heirloom baby crib. The crib was in anticipation of her first grandchild. Jean lived in a very upscale neighborhood, was financially and physically healthy; she had loving adult children, a beautiful home, a faithful loving husband, and a very good life. Yet, she sat and sobbed over what she saw as her daughter's rejection of her. Ultimately, the group raised the issue that the crib was not baby safe, and while a cherished heirloom, was not something a child should sleep in. Jean wasn't happy with that explanation and chose to continue wallowing in her pain for weeks on end, making it much more of an issue than the rest of us thought was reasonable.

I reflected on Jean's very real pain and considered and contrasted what the other members of the group were going through versus what I thought was a ridiculously petty and minor issue. It occurred to me that I, too, got my panties all in a wad over just as minor issues myself now and again. How often have I stewed and fretted over a driver who cut me off in traffic, or felt shame over a busy grocery store clerk who snubbed me, or over poor service at my mechanic's? We all have things that happen to us that, when viewed in a larger or different perspective, are not really all that bad. We make mountains out of molehills.

You may have a devastating illness or be struggling with major issues. I'm not saying those aren't deserving of your attention and pain. I'm saying, keep things in perspective. In the grand scheme of life, is the thing or things you're so obsessed and worried about now going to matter in five years, or even five months?

Don't give in to negativity. It's easy to throw yourself a pity party but resist it as often as possible. If you must wallow in self-pity, limit it to 30 minutes or less. Then find something else to focus on. I wallow, then take a nap, pray, watch a movie, eat, or go for a walk, call a friend or get on YouTube. The longer you focus on the negative things in your life, the more you "feed" them, and the more depressed you'll become.

Avoid seeing crises as insurmountable problems. Change and life happen. You can't change the fact that bad things, stressful things happen, but you can change how you interpret and respond to these events.

Resilience or "grit" is best learned while young, but you can develop it at any age. It's like building muscle. You must build it a little at a time. Practice by following the tips I've just outlined. Do this every day and over time you will see how resilient you become. It won't always be easy, but if you persist, you will get through it.

You're not always going to have the right support, the right friends, the best job, or the skills you need. You're not going to have the money you need, the opportunities you crave, or the environment that you want. You have to learn to do what you can with what you have and keep on going. Ultimately, resilience will bring you through anything you encounter. You just have to believe in yourself. And that, my friend, is the only resilience skill you really need.

https://beckyblanton.com

becky.blanton@gmail.com

PINKK on POINT: Resilience is strong. Strong is kind and powerful. At times we need to be resilient to be kind.

GRATITUDE
BY ATHENA GOLIANIS

"Cultivate the habit of being grateful for every good thing that comes to you, and to give thanks continuously. And because all things have contributed to your advancement, you should include all things in your gratitude." ~ Ralph Waldo Emerson

Unlike empathy, compassion, and caring, gratitude is a learned emotion. It comes from taking time to look at one's life, circumstances, and situation with appreciation.

Gratitude is being aware of and thankful for the good things that happen in your life, no matter how small. It's about taking the time to notice those things, and then to express your appreciation and return the kindness or pass it along as appropriate. Being grateful is more than saying thank you. When you express real gratitude, it can lead to a stronger sense of well-being, self-empowerment, humbleness, and appreciation for life. When we keep a gratitude journal and look for things to be grateful for each day, that practice also teaches us how to be open to opportunities we might not have seen otherwise.

Studies show that when practiced daily, gratitude leads to increased levels of self-esteem, deeper relationships, increased happiness, enhanced well-being, less depression, stronger self-control, better mental and physical health and improved relationships.[2]

Researchers have even found that gratitude increases activity in areas of the brain that deal with morality, reward, and judgment. Gratitude reduces stress; and it helps the body heal faster![3]

FOUNDER & CREATOR'S STORY
GRATITUDE

My dream is to make the world a better and kinder place by empowering and inspiring and creating abundance for women from all walks of life and in doing so make YOUR LIFE BETTER!

I come from a long line of fiercely independent, strong and compassionate women who are the best role models, but I did not want their path. Their world and their times were not easy. So, this is for them and all of that came

---

[2] Miller, Kori D. "14 Health Benefits of Practicing Gratitude According to Science." PositivePsychology.com. March 7, 2019. https://positivepsychology.com/gratitude-appreciation

[3] Miller, Kori D. "14 Health Benefits of Practicing Gratitude According to Science." PositivePsychology.com. March 7, 2019. https://positivepsychology.com/gratitude-appreciation

before, and those that are here now creating and changing things for the better in oh, so many ways.

Change. One thing that we can count on is that the only constant is change. The only one that consistently likes change is a wet baby.

Consider that 50 years ago not a lot of women were in the workforce and relatively few went to college. (No other WOMEN in our family in generations prior were college graduates. I put myself through school with a lot of jobs, scholarships, believers and support of all sorts. I get it.)

No one owned a computer. There were no billionaires. Congress wasn't a version of pro wrestling. There were no cell phones and texts that now allow us immediate access and communication to all - and/or that feeling of burden that we need to check in constantly.

Social media was not there to help hear stories and to tell our stories to all who want to listen - or to be an energy vampire. Pay phones were prevalent and keeping dimes and quarters in your pocket (to call home) still mattered and so on...

So, in another 50 years, what will things be like? What will be the norm? What will we collectively or individually have done to make the world better?

Perhaps the norm is irrelevant. The norm is just average. My grandma, who left this world just 37 days short of 104, would tell you and I agree that there is no "normal." There's simply the continuous cycle of change. And she sure did see more change than most of us. My grandma was not the norm, either. She was ahead of her time for any generation.

And while there is no "normal", together we can always work to change things for the better. We will try. PINKK™ and this is for them, too.

I can hear her now say to my mom and I before she left, "Do not forget your roots. All else might change, but do not forget your roots." So true. I won't, Grandma.

MOM (& a little that I know on Dad)

My mom was widowed, becoming a single mom at age 28. She raised four kids on her own. She never remarried. Besides working full time as a nurse, she also took on double shifts. She was also my Girl Scout leader, room mother, and even president of the Mother's Club. She was always there, time and again for all of us. Yep. She was present and still is always there. It's almost like magic. She is a unicorn and an outlier!

Out of sheer determination (and smarts) she got her bachelor's degree and then a few years later her master's degree at the age of 55 –again working full time with children at home. Not the norm, especially then. Not easy. She was more like a ROCK STAR. She "retired" at the age of 78 and, of course, she still volunteers full time. Hard to find her at home. Coffee (no decaf, please) is her friend.

Growing up, I never really knew when she had time to sleep. Back then, and I shudder to think of this, when a woman (or man, for that matter) left work to have children there was no FMLA (Family Medical Leave Act). That means there was no guarantee that she would have a job upon returning to work. When you are the only breadwinner and a mom, that is bad news. It meant that you must leave your job to have a child, even if not for long. Back then they knocked women out to give birth and that meant a hospital stay was almost always required. So, this could be devastating if you did not get your job back.

She did not stay out of the workplace long, but there was that, plus there weren't lots of jobs for women back then. When women worked outside of the home, traditionally they were teachers or nurses.

The only way I found out about all this was when they were celebrating one of her retirements (she tried a few times, but they kept dragging her back in; or maybe she just did not want to go). But the years of her retirement did not seem quite right. She had to explain the whole s*tarting over* thing again, and how that worked. That just seems unfathomable.

When she left, she was in senior management as she had her master's in Health Administration. She really loved working the floor, and I think she liked third shift the best as there were no "meetings," just the work of taking care of patients. That said, I recall her going back into work countless times for staff meetings, board meetings, admin stuff and paperwork during the day.

One time not that many years ago when my mom was still working, we were home for a weekend visit. We were staying with my grandma, as we often did and this trip she was not feeling well. We called her doctor, who told us to go to the hospital immediately. I remember dropping her off at the entrance where they picked her up in a wheelchair. I parked the car and came back just in time to see my grandma signing into the hospital. Just as I walked towards her, I heard someone say to her, "You're Bev's mom, right?" And then she looked in my direction, smiled and said, "And you must be her daughter, Helena." (No, but I just went along and nodded yes as that seemed the easiest thing to do.)

The next thing I know we are whisked away (grandma in a wheelchair) and me running behind. Then I hear them page my mom. Grandma is in a treatment room with a doctor lickety-split. Just like that.

But Mom did not like this young doctor and in mere moments, got a new one (I was not sure why). It was like she ran the place. The first doctor was dismissed. *Did that happen a lot?* I wondered. At first, I felt kind of sorry for the young doctor, but then not so much as Grandma had issues that needed quick movement, fast decisions, and an excellent assessment and diagnosis. Mom knew exactly who to get to handle all those things, pronto.

Now, this was nepotism of the best and highest order in full action on that day. Grandma and I had a good laugh later about how important we felt. We were also both kind of scared, but this passed. I just thought *I* sure would not mess with Bev when she wants something done. *GET OUT of THE WAY*. We forgot that Mom was there that day when we departed for the hospital rather quickly. Of course, we did not call to bother her as she was working. Indeed, she was, but she was working THERE.

My mom was always working or doing something for someone. That was the case when she met my dad, too. She was picking up her younger sister from school (he was the hot young principal). But her first impression was that he thought too much of himself. When she met him again a couple of months later in a bar (I would have loved to have been there for that) she thought more of the same, until she didn't. He got her. Literally and figuratively. My father became the love of her life, but that did not come without challenges.

Years later, when Dad passed away (via a heart attack), he left no insurance. He had been married before too. My parents were young, so it seems to me in hindsight, they did not plan well for this unthinkable death. In fact, I never knew much about all that happened, but things always have a way of coming out later in my family from unexpected sources. Sometimes things are better left unknown, and then it seems we all want answers.

Dad had been a medic in the Korean War ("Conflict"— ummm, no War). During his tour of duty as a medic in the Navy, he had suffered a heart attack. Yet this fact did not prevent them from trying to enlist him a second time for Vietnam. How did he avoid it? One-word answer. *Death*. Dad died before they could send him back into service. He was 34 years old. Mom was there by his side when he died.

He was a special education teacher. For 45 years, Peoria School District, where he had taught, issued a Teacher of the Year award annually in his name. "The George R. Golianis Award for Outstanding Special Education Teacher is given in memory of Mr. George R. Golianis, a special education teacher, who taught students at Von Steuben School until his death in 1967." The award is based on excellence in teaching and a sincere interest in assisting exceptional children in and beyond the school environment. I think it started in 1968 and ended in 2012.

So why didn't my mom remarry? You would have to ask her, but I think it was not really her path. She married the love of her life. She had a long-term relationship with my uncle, yes, my dad's (divorced) brother (on and off) for many years after my father passed. More scandal to some, and to others, just an accepted family thing to do. Family supporting family. Depends on who you ask. Yet they did not marry. There is a lot more to this story that I am not ready to share here, as I'm not sure it's the right time to do so.

I found it fascinating that after most of us were long gone (me off to school), my uncle did buy the house next to her and lived there for many, many years. But they led separate lives. In a strangely fitting déjà vu kind of way, as with my father, Mom was there by his side when he died. She planned his funeral, too.

I am asked (not so much anymore) did I miss my dad? I guess I miss the idea of him. It is hard to miss what you did not have. The sense of loss is not so pervasive when you never really had something.

That aside, she says I am just like him and that seemed to cause him stress–which I get. The story goes that when he came home from school, he would often choose to drop me off at my grandma's because I just kept following him around in my relentless quest for his attention. One time (allegedly) around the age of almost 4, my mom came home from third shift before he left for school, to find me on the kitchen counter with all the sugar bowls somehow out of the cupboard. I was having a breakfast of white, brown and maybe, family legend has it, even the powdered sugar. Oh, that is the kicker, adding powdered sugar. HA!

When my mom asked if he knew where his daughter was, he responded quickly, "Yes, asleep in bed." To which she responded, "Not that one, your *other* daughter." (My wonderful older sister apparently never did that kind of thing). I am not really buying it. I know I always felt like I had everything I needed; you just had to figure out how to get it, be that sugar or whatever you want that seems to be out of your reach.

I was told and as noted in my baby book I asked *for* Dad, and *about* Dad for a long time. Mom also included the observation that I was a very quiet child for a while— until I wasn't. When I was four, I started asking a lot of questions and have not stopped asking all sorts of questions since then. My siblings and I went to a public grade school for years K-8. I loved it, but my mom says that today, we would not be going there. We did not go to the Catholic school in our parish for grade school then because my sister and I (both born in October) would have had to wait a year to enroll because we were 4 at the beginning of the school year. But the public school accepted us at that age. I know my mom was more than happy to get any of us into school and out of the house.

However, she did insist that each of us go to Catholic High School for at least one year. There were three choices then—Bergan High School, Spalding (boys only), and Academy of Our Lady (girls only). I chose Bergan and graduated from there. That said, I was not excited to go there and leave my childhood neighborhood friends. But that was not an option, so off I went.

Day 1 did not go so well, probably because my "energy" was not so good. I say that in hindsight as an adult, what seems like 100 wise years later. Also, the older kids stereotyped me as a *weakling,* as I was new, fresh and vulnerable that day. On the first day of school, a sophomore girl in the locker room, (and yes, I still know exactly who she is, and she knows who she is, too) threw baby powder in my hair. She was pretty much a bully in both the stereotypical and the very physical real sense of the word. She pushed me around. I then went to my next period (lunch) and got in line at the cafeteria, shaking as I was carrying my tray to a table; literally shaking so that you could see everything shifting precariously as I walked to find a seat. Any seat.

I tried, like we all do at 14, to act like all was okay, just another first day of high school, and then after what seemed like an eternity, I finally sat at a table alone. I was not really trying to do anything other than get through that moment of terror. It did not last long, as two girls (Jamie and Lynda, who knew each other as neighbors, but were strangers to me), came and asked if they could sit with me. I think they saw what happened. We did not really talk about my incident of being bullied, and that was just fine. I probably would have cried, which was not the right thing to do on your debut in high school. But we then became lifelong friends. Just. Like.That.

At a school dance, not so long after that incident (I never told anyone—teachers, or anyone else - not even my mom), the bully approached me and said to me directly how "cool I was that I never told on her or ratted her out," or something like that. I just said, "I do not know what you're talking about," and walked away fast. That was that.

I saw my high school girlfriends at an "unsanctioned" high school reunion here in Chicago in October 2018. While not in touch frequently, they have a special place in my heart forever. I just got a text saying the same to me recently. My heart overflows. Kindness begets kindness. It just does. As for the bully, I was told she has troubles of her own. I continue to send her thoughts and energy of kindness because she needs it. I am surrounded by it and am grateful. The rest of high school was pretty much the opposite of *that day*. Yet it stuck with me because it was the first day that had a real impact on me. All that aside, as it turns out, Mom was right to send us to Catholic high school. I learned a lot about life and about how others lived beyond my neighborhood. I liked what I saw, and then some.

My mom was always trying to do the best thing for us, but I got the feeling she never felt it was enough. But it was. It really, really was, especially in hindsight. Of course, there were things I did not understand or like, but then that is called growing up.

I do recall telling a story at a Christmas dinner at our home recently. We were having a discussion around our favorite meals for dinner when we were growing up. For me, the faves revolved around things like white rice with cinnamon and sugar, and cinnamon pancakes. Mom seemed a little defensive and said something like, "We had meat sometimes, too. We had vegetables and protein." It never occurred to me as a child or even in later years that I was missing something. I remember veggies, and especially bacon and ground hamburger meat in a skillet with onions as a meat fave, too. I mean, what kid misses vegetables, right? Her reaction seemed to me that she thought she did something that was inadequate at the time.

We were eating filet mignon for dinner that current Christmas at my home, so it seemed ironic, but it saddened me that she felt that way about how she had raised us. All those years and she still felt like she had not done her best, when in my mind, she had done far more than anyone else possibly could have. I was not hungry. In that way.

I made a mental note and did not tell her or my grandma that growing up, I usually fed my Sunday dinner pot roast to Daisy, Tiffany or Big Girl or one of our other many dogs over the years. That wouldn't have gone over well then, and probably not so much now, either. We always used cloth napkins back then, so there was no way to hide the meat you didn't want, so to speak. Dogs serve so many purposes in life.

Just about a year ago, over dinner, I asked Mom how she survived so much bad stuff, and not only that, but was always so strong. My husband, John, was there with us. After dinner we were spending time with my grandma (who was closer to leaving us than I realized) and that's when she told me there were more things not to be shared just yet. Grandma died a week or so later after this conversation. My cousin told me at Grandma's graveside last October that, "Your mom has lived through hell." Of course, I was naturally very curious about how she had been so resilient and still was.

In response to my question, Mom said without hesitation, "Well, I always thought someone had it worse than me." Truism. (We only know the tip of it all, so to speak. She does not tell a lot still, but I have unearthed things in later years).

Mom taught me GRATITUDE with a capital G.

GRANDMA

That same grandma (my mom's mom) died shamelessly on my husband's birthday on October 15, 2018, just to be sure we would never forget her—as if! She left this earth just a few days short of 104, as I mentioned. That is even more of a big deal because she was pretty healthy until the end.

When we had to take her to the emergency room that weekend I was home, I rode with her in the ambulance which was upsetting as I felt so helpless. But it was the right thing to do. Even in that ambulance, she asked about the Cubs score. She was present. She also asked almost in the same sentence if she was going to die. I know, right? I answered, "No, Grandma, not today." Not today. *Not today, Grandma*, I repeated in my mind, as if to make sure that was true. Turned out it was.

She kept asking where my husband was. He drove alone and met us at the hospital. He was in the waiting room, watching the Cubs. For some reason (true Cubs fan) she still needed to know if the Cubs were going to win. In response to that question, I said, "I am more confident about how to answer if you are going to die today, and by the way, that's still *no, not today* - than whether or not the Cubs will win today, Grandma."

Even though we FINALLY won the World Series (on my grandma's bucket list for around 100 years), it was always dicey to predict a win for them. It was the Cubs, for goodness' sake, and we had all been through a lot with them over the years. Of course, I did not know if she would or would not make it, but I was not ready to say whether she might die. And I did know she was not ready to go. Yet.

My mom came to the emergency room that day shortly after we called her, but my grandma had not asked for her. But, she did (insistently) want to see my husband and kept asking, "Where is John?" We were just chopped liver that day, as the saying goes (Mom and me, that is). She just knew my mom would be there. Because well, she always was.

Sure enough, Grandma did not die that day. That was the last time my husband saw her alive, though. She blew us kisses from her bed in the emergency room as we left to drive back to Chicago. She died a week and one day later, on John's birthday, as I mentioned. For some reason, I knew that morning that she had left this earth, and I woke up just moments before we got the call. *Happy Birthday, John!* Not. John's brother Peter, who passed in 2002 was born on October 15, too. So now you know that, too. Ouch. Just ouch.

All on her own, Grandma started her own wedding cake business out of her tiny kitchen in Pottstown, IL in the 1950s. She was a very successful baker for over 45 years. Customers called her from CHICAGO to get her to make their wedding cakes. Wedding dates were set around her avails to do the cake. Really.

She was a 'viral marketing' genius before that was a thing, and an 'influencer' before *that* was a thing. What I mean by that is that everyone wanted Alma McCoy to make their wedding cake, and it was all word of mouth. Her expertise spread virally throughout generations of families as well as to one of the biggest employers in Peoria at the time (Caterpillar). Pretty much everyone for miles around knew about her delicious cakes, because she was "IT."

One of my favorite stories is about when one of my dear friends from high school was going to be married in Peoria after college. As soon as I learned that she was getting married in Peoria, I asked if she wanted my grandma to make her wedding cake. She and her mother were as sweet and kind as could be and said, "Oh, thank you so much, but we were able to get Alma McCoy." I smiled inside and said, "Okay, then. I'll let Grandma know." My grandma was Alma McCoy!

Of course, I did not exactly correct them, and when I told Grandma they "got some old lady to make her cake," she just said, "Oh, well, that's nice then…" Exactly when they all sorted out who she was I do not recall. But as a sidebar, this friend had actually met my grandma many times, but as kids, you never talked about that kind of stuff. I mean to say, usually anything about what your grandparents did was boring unless they were famous or rich or something. Clearly, we were not. Not even close. Well, with the exception that in her own way in local circles, Grandma was famous for her cakes.

So, how did Chicago folks start calling her to create their wedding cakes? I think the main reason was that the Chicago Cubs had a farm team in Peoria (the Peoria Chiefs) for many years, and the word spread that way, too. I know for a fact she did Mark Grace's cake, and not sure who else as they may have never made it to the majors. It is an understatement to say she loved her CUBS until the day she died. They loved her, too.

Grandma created demand by limiting supply.

Crazy like a fox, she was. I love hearing stories of when she just said no if someone was not kind or for whatever reason. It was not like she did not need the money, she (we) always did. But it was the "principle of the thing," don't you know? One of the funnier story lines about this is one that by cousin told me at Grandma's graveside, of all places. She told me that when she asked my grandma many years back if she would make her wedding cake, Grandma quickly retorted, "I made you two already. How many more do you need?" So, there was that.

She was doing organic and farm-to-table before it was a "thing," and there was no Whole Foods then. Finally, one boutique small "health food store" came to Peoria (near Pottstown) in the 1970s.

They called her a "health food nut." She would get her eggs from Fryer's farm, and no ingredients were processed or preserved. If she could make it from scratch, she would. Remember, this was the time of big food and convenience and all that. She went against the grain. Not the norm. I just know all that she created was beautiful, and those were the best tasting cakes and baked goods I have ever had. I am not alone. She was ahead of her time! We could never have fast food or anything processed or fake, and this in the time of the fast food explosion, too! We could have Arby's on occasion and Tiger Bars (cocoa bars). I wonder what Arby's did that made them "okay" (Grandma- approved) back then. We never asked, but we sure loved that shaved beef.

Before she married my grandfather, she was married to a man who abused her. (I never met him). She was a beauty, and he was extremely jealous. So, when he went to World War II, she left him. She told me she made him sign up for the draft or else she would leave him. Not sure how that went down, but while he was gone, apparently, she filed for divorce and wrapped that up. I think she had made it clear what was transpiring. On a side note, oddly enough as fate would have it, my mom (as a nurse) was also at my grandma's first husband's bedside when he died. Again, there's more to that story too, but not for this book or maybe ever in writing.

As it turned out, Grandma married my grandfather on Valentine's Day in 1946. He, too, had been married before and in earlier years, he had been her milkman. She married the milkman for real!

When my grandfather died in 1980 (at a young 65) we were all there by his side, other than my sister, as we could not find her in enough time. She was not happy about that for a long time. I was told she was so upset because she really loved him. We all did. My sister also told me that John (my husband) reminded her of Grandpa. I just smiled.

After his death, my grandma was going to quit her business as she did not think she could deliver the wedding cakes by herself. That is, she *tried* to quit. She was done or so she thought. That did not work out as they (her customers) would not let her, and that was a good idea for all involved as it turned out. So, she enlisted us, mostly my youngest brother, to help her deliver the cakes. It all worked out, or at least we never really messed anything up, anyway. She went on to run her business until 1997 or so, I think. She did this alone - without my grandfather, that is - for over 16 years or more.

I also remember that the story of one cake she made where they had asked her to do something different that she had not done before, or tested out yet, anyway. It was something like putting on different kinds of decorations than her usual ones, or something. At any rate, that "special request" made the cake tiers too heavy, so it completely crashed under the weight and fell apart. She stayed up the entire night for over 24 hours straight, baking and recreating the whole thing. These cakes took days and days to create. She would not disappoint the bride, but it was just little old her, so she did what she had to do. She could have farmed it out to one of the bakeries or something, but she would never do that. Or she could have refunded their money and let it go, but she persevered.

I never heard that story until her funeral, either. She never ever complained. Never. Well, except about some family members now and then. She might have called that gossiping rather than complaining neither of which we were allowed to do.

For our wedding, because she could not do our cake (she didn't have all the stuff to do it anymore, and it was just too much to ask), instead she made over 400 heart-shaped hand-painted cookies. They were dipped in chocolate on the back with our names on the front. They were both beautiful and delicious. Each was individually wrapped and tied with a silk ribbon. I saved one for 17 years until someone ate it. *I know who you are.* There are still two of her hand-painted Santa Claus sugar cookies with chocolate in our freezer. I will never eat them. And everybody else - *hands off!*

I remember Sundays at Grandma's with mostly easy, fun, fond memories. We would go to church together (St. Cecilia's) and then go get donuts in the church basement after mass. I recall people looking at my mom and her pile of kids, and could sense they felt awkward, as if something was wrong with us. We were okay and well-behaved as much as any kids are at a certain age. Really, we were not badly behaved—we were too afraid to be, so that was not it. It did seem like that everyone else (Catholics in the later 1960s), all had piles of kids then too, but I could smell it. It was the scent of sadness or something more sinister (pity, judgement) mixed with sticky fingers and glazed donuts (the soft doughy kind). But it was their judgment, not so much the donuts, that gave me a stomachache. It must have given my mom one, too, one too many times, because while we went to church regularly, we often skipped the donuts in the smelly (to me) church basement.

I told my grandma that I did not like those donuts. Maybe she knew why, so we always had something better waiting for us at her house. Always. Remember, she was a baker. Best. Baker. Ever. Ever. Ever.

Sundays consisted of Grandma's house for a big later afternoon dinner, always all homemade from scratch; meat, potatoes, vegetables (multiple) and always, always desert. Grandma waited on all of us. We did not mind. We were spoiled. Afterward, we watched the *Lawrence Welk Show* (oh, those dresses, shoes and Bobby & Sissy) and *Mutual of Omaha's Wild Kingdom* (great sponsor for the magical Marlin Perkins), followed by *The Wonderful World of Disney*. Magic on all fronts.

Dinners together involved lots of conversation about things I did not quite think were logical as a child. Just one example is any conversation about politics. I could go on and on here, but three quick things: 1) My mom (it felt and sounded like to me) was one of maybe five crazy people to vote, or if she did not actually do so, at least considered voting for George McGovern. 2) The President was a "crook." But to my child's mind, how could THE PRESIDENT be a crook? They must be confused. 3) One word: NIXON.

I did go on some years later to run my eighth grade Student Mock Presidential Election. My candidate, Jimmy Carter, won.

I also recall that my grandpa would on occasion have to "run an errand" on Sunday nights for about a half-hour, and sometimes each one of us would get to go with him. Not all of us at once, though. We went down the hill to the Pottstown Tavern and got gum (Wrigley spearmint sticks, the kind in the green package) and he got a beer. I sat on the bar. Yes, *on* the bar. I was little, and it was the perfect perch. All could see me; I was out of the way and I had a great view. When we got home, I would often run back inside through the house to find Grandma, who of course, was almost always in the kitchen. I would say, "I am supposed to remember to tell you that we did not go to the tavern, and send you the message that Mrs. Or Mr. So-and-So says hello to you, Grandma." Never was good at keeping a "secret."

Grandma McCoy was sweet and gentle, kind and fierce all at the same time. I guess she had to be.

As a little girl, I recall as we drove by the Children's Home on Knoxville Avenue, she pointed at it and said we should be grateful for our mother. That if she did not have a good job as a nurse and work so hard for us or (even worse) if she died, we would be left there. I said confidently, "Oh no, Grandma, we would get to live with you." Not so much. She said no, we would go there, so we'd better listen to our mom and help her. We did, and I remember thinking to myself, *be ready to get a job as soon as you can so you can live where you want.*

Gratitude again for my mom, but kind of scary back-assward gratitude. I told my Mom that story about Grandma not so long ago for some reason, and she told me all these years later that it was not true. Not the being grateful part. That was true. Rather, we would have gone to live with her friend Nancy from nursing school. Who knew? Who told? Who asked?

Crazy inspiring, but still not so easy for them. Those two are their own book.

ME and this whole thing. My story, for this book that is about powerful stories of kindness by inspirational women is about my Mom and my grandma. As it is probably for many of us, it's about family. Those two were there for me. Obviously. I hope we all have one or two people that are there for us in our lives. I am so lucky. Really lucky to be so loved by those two powerful and kind women - those two could save the world in my mind. They have saved many in it.

Because of what I have experienced, I am a believer in the three "tions."

INSPIRA*TION*: What **you feel** matters and heals and leads.

EDUCA*TION*: Knowledge is power, and learning (yes, formal education for me was key, and all kinds of "education" outside of formal) is a way to constantly grow and improve.

MOTIVATION: **Do something** with what you feel, what you know, and what you have learned.

Feel, think, and do.

You need all three to succeed. Simple truths to say, but not always easy to live consistently that way.

I had great teachers throughout my journey, and I still do. The real kind of schoolteachers that are paid to do that, and then others you pick up on the way. Or they pick you up. Either way, all good.

When I am in doubt, I go back to gratitude.

Four Ways to Become More Grateful:

Appreciate everything. Don't be picky. Becky Blanton, one of the authors sharing her story in this book, was once homeless and works part-time with the homeless now. She told me a story about going to help an apparently relatively healthy and able young homeless man by buying him shoes, a jacket, and some other items. He was living under bushes with only a backpack to his name and shoes that were wrapped around his feet with rags. She brought him some new sneakers, a jacket, and a few other items. He looked at her with disgust and said he wanted "Nike" (the very popular, but expensive brand of sneakers), not the off-brand shoes she offered.

The jacket, also new, was a $30 jacket from Walmart but he shunned it as well, demanding a brand name. Ultimately, he walked away with his rag-wrapped sneakers and no jacket as she told him she could not afford the costly name brands he demanded. She saw no reason to spend $200 or more on items for him when that money could buy 5 to 10 men and women shoes and jackets. He did not know how to be grateful for what came his way—wanting what he wanted but was unwilling to work for.

When we are grateful for what we have, we often find that we receive more. Think about a time when you gave a child, friend, or coworker, something. It might have been a sandwich, a book, a ride somewhere, or some other small item. Were you more likely to give more to the person who expressed the most appreciation and true gratitude, or to the person who took the item for granted—even if they said thank you? We all love to give to people who are grateful for our gifts, no matter how large or small. The universe, God, or nature, or whatever force that's out there (even if it's just society), tends to reward gratitude with more. And when we recognize things and are grateful, we tend to see more things in our lives for which we are thankful.

Gratitude can be something as simple as being thankful for good weather when your car breaks down or having all the traffic lights turn green when you're running late to a meeting. It can mean having friends who are willing to cook for you or pick up a prescription for you when you're sick. Nothing is too small to deserve gratitude.

Practice Mindfulness. Mindfulness is the simple act of paying attention to the moment. It means being present, not worrying about the future, or thinking about the past. By noticing things rather than reacting to them, we become mindful. To practice mindfulness and gratitude, sit down daily and think through five to ten things you are grateful for. Don't just write it down and move on. The trick to this exercise is that you need to picture the thing in your mind and then feel it. Sit with that feeling of gratitude in your body.

By doing this mindful practice daily, you'll begin to rewire your brain and feel the difference in 90 days or less. Studies have shown that people start showing a change in brain patterns in as little as eight weeks and start feeling happier in as little as two weeks.

Keep a Gratitude Journal. That's right. Write it down. There's a special connection between the brain and handwriting something in a journal. By journaling, you reinforce your gratitude, and start reshaping your brain's neural pathways. The journal can be as simple or elaborate as you like. A spiral notebook like we used in school, or something more elaborate and ornate work equally well.

I had the pleasure many years ago being part of the team that created gratitude journals for *The Secret*. There was a gratitude quote on each page that inspired each day. It stuck with me. I express gratitude to Rhonda Byrne and

Bob and Margaret Rainone for the gift of participating in that journey with them and *The Secret*. A gift of enduring friendship on so many levels. I know of one woman who writes her gratitude notes on Post-it's and sticks them to her office walls. As she looks around each day, she is surrounded, literally, by all the things she's grateful for!

Express Your Gratitude to Others. It's not just enough to keep your gratitude in a journal. Share it. If someone has done something for you, express your gratitude. If a stranger holds a door open for you, don't just mumble "Thank you," and walk on through. Take a few extra seconds to stop, look the person in the eye, smile and say, "Thank you. I really appreciate your taking the time to do that." It makes a huge difference. Not only have you connected with someone, but you've reinforced their decision to help someone else. Don't forget to send thank you notes.

It's so easy to text or email someone, and it's okay to do that. But think about the last time you got a handwritten thank you note in the mail. It takes expressing your gratitude to others to a whole new level. If someone has introduced someone to you that turns out to be a good connection, let them know. You don't have to write a book but tell the person how things turned out. For instance, "Thank you for introducing me to _____ . It turns out we have so much in common and we are getting together for lunch to discuss how we can help each other!" Just let the person know you are grateful and include a specific example.

How about let's all just be kinder to one another? Women be kinder. Men be kinder. All be kinder to children and animals.

Let's keep at it and lead with heartfelt kindness. That is all we can really do. Kindness begets kindness.

To quote Nelson Mandela: "*It always seems impossible until it's done!*"

PINKK on POINT: Let's remember that kindness grows from gratitude.

EPILOGUE

So here we are making positive change happening by sharing stories to inspire. This book is meant to be for thought leaders just starting out and those who are seasoned. Through the compelling stories here we hope to both connect and teach. I believe strongly that thought leadership through telling stories is a powerful way to inspire positive change.

Now that you have read enough stories to fill you up with your own ideas of what it means to *fly by the seat of your skirt*, what will you do differently?

Here are some starter truths that will help you move forward:

- We will succeed with authenticity, resilience and gratitude!
- We will reach those who want to be a part of this new world where women help one another daily through our collective spiritual, relevant, practical ways.
- We appeal to women based on their affirmations and our kindness.
- Everything emanates from constant appreciation of life with its ups and downs. And this affirms our connection to each other. It also deepens our spirit…. And as we expand our appreciation, we make a difference in the world.

- We need to GIVE BACK not GIVE UP and share kindness with the world.
- We all have a story. We all may not look like our story. The only way to be true is to tell our own story and truth.

Thank you!

Thank you for joining us on this flight of Kindness. We trust that you have enjoyed the stops along the way and have been reminded of those acts of kindness where you have been both the recipient and benefactor. We also hope that you are motivated to continue practicing kindness and paying it forward in a mindful, caring way on a daily basis. We believe you'll agree there's no better feeling in the world.

It's been a pleasure and honor to share our stories with you. We encourage you to take flight via the wings of your own passionate cause(s) and spread kindness all along the way. The world needs as much positivity as possible right now, and yes, one by one, by owning our responsibility to the planet and one another and by including kindness in our daily agenda, our individual lights will unite to shine brightly throughout the universe. Fly high and the winds and wings of kindness will always buoy you up.

ABOUT THE AUTHOR

A thena Golianis Walker currently resides in Chicago, Illinois with her husband, John F. Walker. She is Founder and President of AGW Idea Group, Inc. a marketing consulting and branding agency and is Founder and Creator of PINKK™. PINKK is focused on helping women from all walks of life create and experience a kinder world.

Her goal through PINKK™ is to help women tap into their *real voices* so they can make more and better choices, embracing a new paradigm she calls the "Female Renaissance."

She is a native of Peoria, Illinois and has her Bachelor's in Advertising and PR from Drake University School of Journalism, where she graduated magna cum laude. She has her Master of Science in Advertising from the Northwestern University Medill School of Journalism

She welcomes the opportunity to help companies and brands and all of you to tell your powerful stories.

www.AGWideaGroup.com

www.pinkknow.com

ABOUT THE COVER

The cover was created by Isabella Vonachen, a native of Peoria, Illinois who recently graduated from the University of Dayton, and started her career in Chicago as a graphic artist. The author believes in promoting young women on their journeys and selected this young artist from her hometown to do just that.

GIVING BACK

PINKK™ starts with our collective *power* bringing us together.

It's about *inspiring* us all to do more and be better, and to make the world a better place today and for the future.

It's a *network* of women committed to network, mentor, coach and contribute to learning from one another, and providing *knowledge* to others from our paths and our experiences. Knowledge is power. Shared, it can become impactful at all levels.

Done with heartfelt *kindness* and trust we can help provide security and contribute to changing women's lives for the better.

With PINKK™ done right, one need not ask nor put out their hand because they each have something the other wants and can give!

BEFORE YOU GO

Thank you so much for allowing me to spend time with you as you read this book. I'd like to take just a few more minutes to make a couple of simple requests.

If you enjoyed this book or gained even one insight that's helpful to you, please share this with others. Are there others in your network that would potentially benefit from reading *Flying by the Seats of Their Skirts*? I invite you to share your learnings with them.

Also, would you be so kind as to take a moment, go to Amazon (www.amazon.com), look up the title, *Flying by the Seats of Their Skirts* and leave a short review? Even if you only have time to go through a couple of chapters, it would still be helpful to leave a review. Your impressions and takeaways are useful in helping other leaders like yourself find this resource.

In our content-cluttered world, books succeed by the kind, generous time readers take to leave honest reviews. I thank you in advance for this very kind gesture of appreciation. It means the world to me and my author contributors.

Join us @ www.pinkknow.com

Contact: Info@pinkknow.com

Info@AGWIdeaGroup.com

www.AGWIdeaGroup.com

Finally, Melissa G Wilson, my publishing partner, is offering you the gift of her best-selling *Networlding Guidebook* (a top ten Amazon book for an entire year) in a pdf format, If you want to start your own circle of support and giving to make your own special difference in the world, just email her at melissa@networlding.com with your request.

ACKNOWLEDGMENTS

First, I thank my husband, John. F. Walker, the love of my life and a gift of immeasurable kindness to me and to the world.

Also, thanks to my family, especially my mom, Beverly A. Golianis. She is strength and compassion and a natural-born nurturer and lover of all creatures - humans included. She never gave up in the face of adversity. She is a rock of stability in a sometimes-rocky world.

Thank you to my grandma, Alma M. McCoy, a self-taught genius and powerful creative force and small businesswoman, a fierce trailblazer with only a 8th grade education. I miss you every single day, Grandma.

Finally, thank you to my publishing partner, Melissa G Wilson, and to all the brave, beautiful and kind women who contributed to this book. We will soar together!